W9-CRJ-690

# THE FOUNDATIONS OF DUAL LANGUAGE INSTRUCTION

## Judith Lessow-Hurley
San Jose State University

*lengua*

*langue*

*sprache*

*lingua*

*langue*

Longman *Publishers USA*

**The Foundations of Dual Language Instruction,** Second Edition

Longman, 10 Bank Street, White Plains, N.Y. 10606

Associated companies:
Longman Group Ltd., London
Longman Cheshire Pty., Melbourne
Longman Paul Pty., Auckland
Copp Clark Longman Ltd., Toronto

Production editor: Linda Moser/York Production Services
Editorial assistant: Matt Baker
Cover design: Lisa Delgado, Delgado Design
Compositor: Execustaff

**Library of Congress Cataloging-in-Publication Data**
Lessow-Hurley, Judith.
    The foundations of dual language instruction / Judith Lessow-
Hurley.—2nd ed.
        p.   cm.
    Includes bibliographical references.
    ISBN 0-8013-1556-5
    1. Education, Bilingual.   2. Language and languages.   I. Title.
LC3715.L47   1996
3471.97—dc20                                              95-16859
                                                              CIP

5 6 7 8 9 10-MA-999897

To my father, who encouraged me to learn two languages

# Contents

**v**

## CHAPTER 5  **LANGUAGE ABILITY**    51

## CHAPTER 6  **PRIMARY LANGUAGE INSTRUCTION FOR LIMITED ENGLISH PROFICIENT STUDENTS**    61

# Preface

Education in more than one language has many historical precedents and is necessary and common around the world today. Population changes in the United States are resulting in a virtual flood of public school children whose needs cannot be met without dual language instruction. In addition, our national economic welfare and political security require that we prepare all children with more than one language so they can cope with a shrinking world and an interdependent global economy. Dual language instruction should be, therefore, a routine component of schooling for every child. This book is a basic text for teachers in training. It is not a book about methodology. The term *bilingual methods* is in itself misleading and often gives rise to confusion and misconstruction. There are, after all, no "bilingual" tangrams, math blocks, or even books or activity sheets.

In the normal course of instructional events, all competent teachers can design objectives, organize materials, structure activities, and devise evaluation strategies. Any good teacher doing those things can answer the questions: "What are you doing?" and "Why are you doing that?" A dual language classroom teacher performs the same tasks but must also include language as a variable in all aspects of planning.

*What* and *why* are basic questions for all teachers, but the dual language teacher must answer an additional and difficult question: "What language are you using to teach each particular child, at any given time, in any particular subject?" While this question is methodological in part, the answer results not only from the nature of the task at hand but also from an interplay of theoretical knowledge about language and culture, state and federal mandates, and administrative decisions about program design.

The foundations of dual language instruction comprise, therefore, a complex mosaic involving theory, research, and discourse from several different areas of scholarship and inquiry. To understand how language works in an educational setting, it must be objectified and identified as a tool to be manipulated for instructional purposes, much as we manipulate books, maps, and other instructional aids. To develop this awareness, we must turn to linguistics for information about the nature of language; to psycholinguistics for information about language and the mind; to sociolinguistics for information about how language works in society; and to psychology, sociology, and anthropology for insights into human interaction and culture.

The purposes of this book are twofold and may at first appear to be contradictory. First, dual language instruction must be removed from its controversial political environment. Misinformation about dual language instruction permeates the public mind and, all too often, the teaching profession itself.

Opposition to bilingual education is the result of several common misconceptions. The first misconception relates to time. Schooling in general, and language learning in particular, are slow processes. Preoccupied, as we are in the post-modern era, with speed, we are often impatient with educational programs that do not yield overnight results. But human development proceeds at its usual pace, regardless of changes in technology that result in speed and cost savings in other areas of endeavor. It takes time to develop proficiency in a language and particularly to reach a level of competence adequate to the demands of schooling. All too often, programs are judged on results obtained in two or three years—and it's not surprising that such results fail to demonstrate dramatic success.

Second, many people regard language learning as a difficult and frustrating endeavor. This attitude is usually the result of having experienced traditional, grammar-based approaches to language teaching. It is common to hear people say, "I took three years of French (or Spanish, or German) in high school, and I can't speak a word." Most of the people who say that would like to speak another language, but the main thing they learned from language class is that it's hard to do! It's not surprising that they are skeptical about the possibility that an educational program can produce bilingualism without pain.

Finally, and perhaps most dynamically, using languages other than English in public schools empowers minority communities and provides marginalized or excluded groups with a voice in schooling. Despite constant demands for reform in schooling, most of us resist change: alterations in the status quo—in schools and society—albeit for the better, are disquieting. Bilingual education has become a flash point in the current political climate which targets minorities and attempts to blame them for a host of social and economic woes.

So the first item of business for this book is to take an unemotional look at dual language instruction and examine its component parts in a scholarly fashion. Having done that, however, we must next reinsert it into the social environment and develop an understanding of the politics of dual language instruction and the controversy it inspires.

Many people are surprised to learn that bilingual environments are common around the world and that learning in more than one language is the norm rather than the exception. In the United States, dual language instruction is not at all new, having enjoyed a significant period of popularity in the nineteenth century. Chapter 1 presents a historical and international overview of bilingualism and dual language education and sets the stage for later discussions of politics and policy. Chapter 2 explains the concept of a program model, details the different models prevalent in the United States today, and describes the competencies required of dual language educators. This chapter also clarifies the distinction between bilingual and multicultural education.

Language is as essential to us as the air we breathe and is equally invisible. On one hand, it is difficult to see; on the other, it is a source of powerful emotion. Because teachers need an objective understanding of language and of bilingualism, Chapters 3, 4, and 5 are devoted to fundamental aspects of language. As a starting point in the process of creating a vision of language as an instructional tool, Chapter 3 offers a definition of language and description of its subsystems. And because discussion of language is so often obscured by attitudes, biases, and emotional attachments, the chapter analyzes and attempts to defuse people's common language biases. Strategies for teaching languages must be based on what we know about how languages are learned. Chapter 4 reviews current theories of first language development and second language acquisition. Chapter 5 describes language ability, explains how it can be assessed, and includes a discussion of bilingualism in individuals.

While no one seems to deny that knowing more than one language is beneficial for children whose first language is English, controversy surrounds the idea of providing first language instruction for limited English proficient children in the United States. Chapter 6 develops a five-point rationale for providing primary language instruction to limited English proficient children, emphasizing the work of Jim Cummins, whose analysis of school-related proficiency has laid much of the groundwork for current thinking in this area. In addition, Chapter 6 describes approaches for providing primary language support in the classroom, depending on program models.

Many program models include some type of direct second language instruction. Chapter 7 discusses the historical development of several approaches to second language instruction and recent innovations in the field. Also included are discussions of specially designed academic instruction in English, which simultaneously addresses content instruction, second language development, and the development of literacy and biliteracy.

Language is a natural focus for the study of dual language instruction, but language is inextricably tied to culture. The increasing heterogeneity of our school population demands increasing attention to cultural diversity. Many school administrators and classroom teachers make a sincere attempt to respond to ethnic diversity through holiday observances, inclusion of ethnic foods in school menus, and selection of materials that reflect different life-styles. Although positive, these well-intentioned responses to diversity remain essentially superficial.

A culturally responsive classroom must reach beyond surface or artifact culture and attend to the basic differences in the way children from different backgrounds understand, communicate, and learn. Teachers must understand the nature of culture, its relationship to language, and the relationship of specific cultures to the culture of American schools. Chapter 8 outlines a definition of culture, giving examples of its characteristics and manifestations. Chapter 9 describes four analyses of the relationships between culture and school achievement, with emphasis on the contextual interaction model and the recent work of John Ogbu and Carlos Cortés.

Dual language instruction requires educational planning that is not only based on theoretical considerations but that is also within the framework of federal and state law. Chapter 10 reviews the legislative and judicial foundations of dual language instruction, with special attention to the federal Bilingual Education Act (Title VII), the U.S. Supreme Court's 1974 decision in *Lau v. Nichols,* and subsequent legislation and case law.

Finally, all schooling in the United States takes place in a political context. Dual language instruction manipulates language and culture for instructional purposes. The emotional relationships that people have to language and culture result in a particularly charged reaction to bilingual education. The last chapter analyzes the politics of bilingualism and discusses language and its relationship to the ideas and ideals of American identity.

As a text for teachers in training, this book is intended to be simple; given the scope of the subject, it is necessarily superficial in many areas. With this in mind, annotated suggestions for further reading have been included at the end of each chapter, so that readers may pursue their particular interests in depth. In addition, each chapter is followed by questions for thought and suggested hands-on activities to provide students with first-hand insights into and experience in the concepts presented.

While this book attempts to provide an objective review of theory, research, and practice in dual language instruction, the reader will quickly note that I have a strong bias. When I started teaching in a bilingual demonstration program in the late 1960s, our program provided Spanish instruction for monolingual English-speaking children of all backgrounds and Spanish maintenance with English as a second language for Hispanic children whose English was limited. Our program had a strong community base and moved effectively toward the goal of making all our children bilingual and biliterate in English and Spanish.

It is ironic that the growing legislative support we hoped for was the undoing of programs such as ours. Faced with mandates for services for large numbers of limited English proficient children, school districts decided that two-way programs (as they are now called) were a dispensable luxury. There can be no doubt that the needs of limited English proficient children are an immediate first-order priority. But until we inculcate an understanding of the value of bilingualism in the general population, such programs will always be vulnerable and insecure. As a bilingual person and a bilingual teacher, it is my unshakable conviction that dual language instruction benefits all children.

## ACKNOWLEDGMENTS

I would like to extend my gratitude to the following individuals who served as reviewers for the second edition of this text:

Alfredo H. Benavides, Arizona State University
Kimberley Brown, Portland State University
Istvan Kecskes, University of Montana
Paul Markham, University of Kansas
Mary McGroarty, Northern Arizona University
Holli Schauber, University of Cincinnati
Milagros M. Seda, University of Texas at El Paso
Maureen Siera, Eastern Washington University
Meritt Stark Jr., Henderson State University

In addition, I would like to thank my colleagues in the bilingual education community for their support and encouragement, and my husband—for everything.

chapter **1**

# Historical and International Perspectives

**P**eople from the United States are sometimes surprised to find that tourists and immigrants often speak, read, and write several languages. Around the world, bilingualism is more the norm than the exception. This is true now and also has been true historically. In this chapter we review the history of bilingualism and dual language education around the world and consider examples of the use of two languages in today's society and in education.

## SOCIETAL BILINGUALISM

### The Ancient World

Bilingualism was common in antiquity. Political and territorial consolidation and domination of one or more groups of people by others generally created situations in which conquered groups added the dominant language to their repertoire. Ancient conquerors' linguistic tolerance favored linguistic diversity. Starting in the sixth century B.C.E., ancient Greeks, for example, penetrated and dominated large areas of the Mediterranean. While they preserved and promulgated Greek language and culture through schooling, they had no interest in replacing local languages with their own. With language shifts slow in the making, many individuals maintained the ability to function in more than one language (Lewis, 1976).

To the extent that formal schooling was available, education in more than one language seems to have been the norm in the ancient world. The need for dual language education may have been tied to literacy. The scarcity of written materials meant that a person who wanted to read widely had to read in more than one language (Mackey, 1978).

**1**

Education in Europe always has placed value on bilingualism and biliteracy—dating back to the Romans who implemented formal schooling on a large scale throughout their empire and schooled all students in Latin regardless of their first language. Latin as the language of schooling persisted until relatively recently, when the rise of nationalism and the concurrent Protestant Reformation motivated the use of vernaculars for scholarship and education.

## Bilingualism among Jews

Jewish bilingualism from ancient times to the present has received the special attention of scholars (Lewis, 1976). Jews used Hebrew for worship long after it ceased to be a mainstream Jewish language. Dispersed around the world, Jews have learned many languages while simultaneously maintaining a home or community language. Although no longer widely spoken, Yiddish is perhaps the most familiar Jewish language to English speakers, since it is related to German. As you can see in the list below, many Yiddish words and constructions have entered English usage:

> *bagel:* a bread, shaped like a donut, that is boiled and then baked
>
> *chutzpah:* nerve or audacity
>
> *glitch:* an unexplained malfunction; usually refers to computer programs
>
> *klutz:* a clumsy person (adjective: *klutzy*)
>
> *maven:* an expert; sometimes slightly pejorative—a know-it-all
>
> *schlock:* cheap or badly made merchandise (adjective: schlocky)
>
> *schmaltz:* over-flowery sentiment (adjective: *schmaltzy*)

It is interesting to note that there is still a significant population of Sephardic Jews who speak Ladino, a form of Spanish spoken by Jews of Greek, Turkish, and Syrian ancestry and written with the Hebrew alphabet. Spanish was carried to the Middle East by Spanish and Portuguese Jews exiled from Spain in the late fifteenth century.

## The Modern World

Bilingualism is common in modern times in almost every corner of the world. In 1982, Grosjean suggested that only Japan and what was then West Germany could be classified as monolingual countries, and even they had significant populations whose first language was not the language of the majority. In general, we live in a multilingual world.

There are many officially monolingual nations that house large linguistic minorities. This is especially characteristic of newly independent developing nations whose political boundaries do not coincide with linguistic boundaries and who have chosen a national language for unification purposes.

A number of countries are officially bilingual or multilingual, including Canada, Belgium, Finland, Cyprus, Israel, Ireland, and Czechoslovakia. Note that official bilingualism does not imply that all inhabitants of a country are bilingual. Often only a small percentage of the population of an officially bilingual country uses both languages regularly. Official bilingualism means that more than one language may be used in transactions with the government or in the schools. Different countries develop different policies with respect to the languages they endorse.

Some countries may have many more languages than their governmental policies recognize. Hindi is the official language of India. Although it is the most widely used, 14 other languages plus English are officially recognized in the constitution—these being only a fraction of the 200 different languages spoken on the subcontinent (Kubchandani, 1978).

China is a nation with enormous territory and diverse cultural groups which has many languages represented within its boundaries. Government support for Chinese as a unifying national language, combined with tolerance for diversity, has favored bilingualism.

A discussion of bilingualism in the world would be incomplete without mentioning Paraguay's unique situation. Guarani, the indigenous Indian language of Paraguay, is the national language and the primary language of 90 percent of Paraguay's population. Spanish is Paraguay's official language, used in schools and for other government activities. Over half the population is bilingual, but Guarani—a cherished national treasure—is the language of choice for personal intimacy and poetry (Rubin, 1972).

Language policies invariably reflect political realities. Dramatic changes in government in South Africa, for example, have led to the recognition of nine African languages as official, in addition to English and Afrikaans (National Public Radio, 1995).

## Multilingualism in the United States

When the U.S. Constitution was written, its authors made an affirmative decision not to establish an official national language. Recently, local initiatives have resulted in policies proclaiming the official standing of English. Nevertheless, the United States is a multilingual nation, with many indigenous Native American languages, indigenous Spanish, and the diverse languages of its many immigrant groups, which contribute to the nation's linguistic wealth. (Language policy in the United States is more fully discussed in Chapter 11.)

## EDUCATION IN MORE THAN ONE LANGUAGE: AN INTERNATIONAL PERSPECTIVE

Societal bilingualism is common, and dual language instruction is practiced worldwide. Formats for providing education in two languages are as varied as the world's governments and their constituencies. The following paragraphs describe three cases where governments support more than one language through education.

## Sweden

Bilingual education is provided for immigrant children in Sweden with the goal of enabling them to function fully both in Swedish and their home languages. Children receive all instruction in the home language. Swedish is taught initially as a foreign language, but its use is increased until, by the fifth or sixth grade, instruction in all subject areas is bilingual ("Bilingual programs in Sweden . . . ," 1985).

## China

China has taken steps to preserve its minority languages. Writing systems have been developed for many indigenous languages that previously did not have them. Media broadcasts are often bilingual, and political information is disseminated in a variety of languages (Fincher, 1978). China currently offers home-language instruction to many of its ethnic minorities, with gradual introduction to Chinese in the second year of schooling. Chinese authorities have reported an increase in achievement as well as improved attendance by ethnic minority children enrolled in dual language programs (Wang, 1986).

## Canada

Since the passage of the Official Languages Act in 1967, Canada has been officially bilingual (English and French). The history of bilingual education in Canada is primarily the history of the struggle for equal status for French, which is the minority language. Canada has had notable success with its French-English immersion programs for Anglophones (English speakers), which have provided a model for dual language instruction worldwide. (Immersion programs are discussed in detail in Chapter 5.)

Canada continues to struggle with the needs of speakers of so-called heritage languages—languages other than French and English used by indigenous or immigrant minorities. A variety of dual language instructional programs have been established, some with the goal of transitioning children from their primary languages to English and others with the intention of preserving or restoring proficiency in a heritage language. (For a detailed review of dual language programs for heritage languages in Canada, see Cummins, 1984b.)

## THE HISTORY OF DUAL LANGUAGE INSTRUCTION IN THE UNITED STATES

People are often surprised to discover that dual language instruction has been widely available in the United States since the beginning of its history as a nation. Immigration has been a constant in U.S. history, and languages other than English have been tolerated and even officially recognized from the outset. The Continental

Congress, for example, published a number of documents in German to assure accessibility for the large German-speaking minority (Keller & Van Hooft, 1982).

## The Nineteenth Century

In the nineteenth century, non-English or dual language instruction was offered in more than a dozen states in a variety of languages including German, Swedish, Norwegian, Danish, Dutch, Polish, Italian, Czech, French, and Spanish (Ovando & Collier, 1985; Tyack, 1974). Both immigrants and Native Americans made instruction in two languages available for their children.

*Dual Language Instruction for Native Americans.* Formal schooling was locally administered by Native Americans only insofar as the U.S. government allowed. Where locally controlled education was permitted, Native American communities often provided dual language instruction:

> The Cherokees established and operated an educational system of 21 schools and two academies, which enrolled eleven hundred pupils, and produced a population ninety percent literate in its native language. They used bilingual materials to such an extent that by 1852 Oklahoma Cherokees had a higher English literacy level than the White populations of either Texas or Arkansas. (Castellanos, 1983, p. 17)

The tribes of the southeast were particularly successful in dealing with culture contact with Europeans, who called them the "civilized tribes" as a result. The European perception that the southeastern tribes were capable of self-government resulted in some measure of tribal autonomy in education. In addition, several of the southeastern Indian languages had or developed writing systems, softening the dominance of English and facilitating the availability of dual language education. In general, however, U.S. government tolerance for Native American self-determination, education, and language was tied to political expediency, and those Indian school systems that were permitted to exist and that survived the Civil War were eradicated in the latter part of the nineteenth century (Weinberg, 1977).

*Dual Language Instruction for Immigrants.* Immigrant Germans fared well in maintaining their language through dual language instruction during the nineteenth century. German patriotism in the Revolutionary War was highly regarded, and, therefore, German language and culture were accepted with tolerance. Also, despite the fact that Germans were a minority, they were heavily concentrated in the remote farming areas of the Midwest. As a result of their geographic isolation, they were not viewed as a threat by the rest of the population. Given that education was locally controlled and financed, their concentration enabled them to exert the political strength of their numbers on the schools (Liebowitz, 1978).

In response to political pressure from the German community, German-English dual language programs were instituted in Ohio in 1840; by the turn of the century, 17,584 students were studying German in dual language programs, the great majority of them in the primary grades. Dual language programs were also widespread in Missouri (Tyack, 1974). In 1880 German was taught in 52 of the 57 public schools in Saint Louis, and German-English programs attracted not only German children, but also Anglo American children who learned German as a second language (Escamilla, 1980).

Toward the end of the nineteenth century, anti-Catholic bias provoked by an influx of Irish immigrants spilled over onto previously tolerated Germans, many of whom were Catholic. Increasing immigration resulted in a wave of xenophobia that often targeted foreign languages. The large instructional programs in German gave the language a high profile, and the German language became a focus for the anti-foreign feelings that flourished in the second half of the eighteenth century.

The onset of World War I brought anti-German feeling to a head, and a rash of legislation aimed at eliminating German language instruction caused the collapse of dual language programs around the country. At the turn of the century, only 14 of the 45 states mandated English as the sole language of instruction in the schools. By 1923, a total of 34 of the 48 states had English-only instructional policies (Castellanos, 1983).

## The Twentieth Century

Two byproducts of World War I, isolationism and nationalism, took their toll on dual language as well as foreign language instruction. Instruction in foreign languages was virtually eliminated in the period between the first and second world wars. Events in the 1950s, however, revitalized interest in these fields. The successful launching of Sputnik by the Soviet Union caused a reevaluation of education in general and inspired the National Defense Education Act (1958). Knowledge of foreign languages was perceived as essential to our national defense, so the act provided funding for foreign language study.

During the same period, the Cuban revolution (1958) brought a flood of educated Cuban refugees to Florida. In 1963, in response to the needs of the Cuban community, the Coral Way Elementary School in Dade County, Florida, was established. Coral Way offered dual language instruction for both Cuban and non-Hispanic children. The program served a middle-class population, was well funded from both public and private sources, and—unlike many subsequent programs—was neither compensatory nor remedial.

The nation was in the midst of an energetic movement favoring the expansion of civil rights, accompanied by a powerful affirmation of ethnic identity for minority groups. In that political climate, and with the success of Coral Way in the public eye, bilingual programs were quickly established in a number of states, including Texas, California, New Mexico, New Jersey, and Arizona (Ambert & Melendez, 1985).

In 1965 the Elementary and Secondary Education Act (ESEA) was approved and funded by Congress. The act was part of President Lyndon B. Johnson's War on Poverty, and its broad purpose was to equalize educational opportunities. The Bilingual Education Act, or Title VII of the ESEA, was signed into law in 1968. Title VII did not mandate bilingual education but provided funds for districts to establish programs that used primary language instruction to assist limited English proficient children. In subsequent amendments to the act, funds were allocated for teacher training, research, information dissemination, and program support. (Title VII and other pertinent legislation are discussed in detail in Chapter 10.)

In addition, judicial action provided strong support for services for limited English proficient children. In 1974, the U.S. Supreme Court decision in *Lau v. Nichols* held, on the basis of Title VI of the Civil Rights Act (1964), that children must receive equal access to education regardless of their inability to speak English. (*Lau* and other pertinent decisions are discussed in detail in Chapter 10.)

In 1971, Massachusetts was the first state to mandate bilingual education. By 1983, bilingual education was permitted in all 50 states, and 9 states had laws requiring some form of dual language instruction for students with limited English proficiency (Ovando & Collier, 1985).

In the 1980s lack of government support for primary language instruction, combined with strong reactions to the influx of immigrants, weakened support for dual language instruction. California, for example, with a population of over 1,200,000 limited English proficient children at the present time, allowed its bilingual education law to lapse in June 1987.

Nevertheless, ever-increasing numbers of immigrants from all over the world ensure a continued demand for teachers with skills to work with limited English proficient students. In addition, experiments in dual language instruction in an enrichment mode may broaden the general public's understanding of the value of an education in more than one language.

## SUMMARY

Dual language instruction in one form or another has been available all over the world since ancient times. Countries in the world today may espouse one of many potential language policies, but in any case, there are bilingual individuals in virtually every nation in the world. Dual language instruction is available in many countries in a variety of formats, depending on the population and the purpose.

Dual language instruction has been available in the United States since before colonial times. Nationalistic feelings that accompanied World War I limited the use of languages other than English in schools, but interest in foreign language instruction was revived after World War II. The success of bilingual programs established in Florida shortly after the Cuban revolution, combined with a political climate that favored ethnic identity and civil rights, inspired the implementation of dual language programs nationwide.

## ACTIVITIES AND QUESTIONS TO THINK ABOUT

1. Interview classmates or acquaintances born or educated outside the United States. Find out how many languages they know and how they learned them. If they attended school outside the United States, find out the following:

   Was the language of schooling the same as the home language?

   Were they required to learn more than one language at school?

   Which languages were used for content instruction?

   In their view, how common is bilingualism in the country they came from or studied in?

   Compare their language experiences to your own.

2. Dual language instruction was widespread in the nineteenth century. Look into the history of your area and find out if there were educational programs in more than one language prior to 1963.

3. Many languages are spoken in the United States. Make a language map of your area. Depending on where you live, you may want to map your city, town, or county. A rigorous demographic study may be impractical, but school district figures may be a good starting point. Churches that announce services in various languages may help you. Concentration of ethnic businesses is another clue.

4. Inventory the non-English media in your area. Include radio, television, movies, and newspapers. Check the local public library to find out the number and circulation of non-English materials.

## SUGGESTIONS FOR FURTHER READING

Castellanos, D. (1983). *The best of two worlds: Bilingual-bicultural education in the U.S.* Trenton, NJ: New Jersey State Department of Education.
   Providing a comprehensive look at language policy in the United States, this book analyzes bilingual education from historical, legal, and social perspectives.

Crawford, J. (1989). *Bilingual education: History, politics, theory, and practice.* Trenton, NJ: Crane.
   One of the more comprehensive overview of issues related to bilingual education in the United States, this well-written book provides a detailed analysis of the history and politics of dual language instruction.

Keller, G. D., & Van Hooft, K. S. (1982). A chronology of bilingualism and bilingual education in the United States. In J. A. Fishman & G. D. Keller (Eds.) (1982), *Bilingual Education for Hispanic Students in the United States.* New York: Teachers College Press.
   A chronology of bilingual education in the United States beginning with the colonial period and ending in 1980 with the creation of the Department of Education Office of Bilingual Languages and Minority Language Affairs. There have been many political changes in the last 15 years that have had a dynamic effect on bilingual education, but this book provides an excellent historical record and reminds us that bilingual education is not a new idea in the United States.

Kloss, H. (1977). *The American bilingual tradition.* Rowley, MA: Newbury House.
An analysis of language policy in the United States and its possessions and pro-
tectorates, this book is a classic history of bilingualism and bilingual education and is
generally considered a basic source of information in this relatively unexplored area.
Spolsky, B., & Cooper, R. L. (Eds.). (1978). *Case studies in bilingual education.* Rowley,
MA: Newbury House.
The articles in this collection include a section on national perspectives with descriptions
of bilingual programs in a variety of settings around the world, including Belgium,
Canada, China, India, New Zealand, South Africa, the Soviet Union, and Wales. The
section on social perspectives addresses issues related to bilingual education and
bilingualism around the world.

# chapter 2

# Dual Language Program Models

Simply stated, dual language instruction is an educational program offered in two languages. This definition is straightforward but lacks specificity. Dual language instruction can be offered in a variety of formats or models, depending on the goals of a program and the population it serves.

Some programs, for example, are designed to promote bilingualism and biliteracy for students. Others use a primary or home language as a bridge to assist students while they learn the dominant mainstream language.

This chapter will explain the concept of a program model and describe various types of programs currently in use in the United States. It also presents an overview of the competencies that teachers and paraprofessionals must have to provide instruction in dual language classrooms. Finally, it will clarify the distinction between bilingual and multicultural education and identify the ways they differ and the features they share.

## WHAT IS A PROGRAM MODEL?

If you were to visit a dual language classroom, you might note several features, including the functional use of each language and the methodology for distributing the languages in the curriculum. You would also probably consider the amount of time each language is used. In a particular classroom, you might observe that Spanish is used for instruction 50 percent of the day. Such an observation, however, takes on meaning only in the context of a program model. A *program model* refers to the span of language use and distribution towards a goal for a specific population, across the grades.

If, for example, the classroom you have visited is a Spanish-English bilingual kindergarten, it would be important to know whether the 50–50 time distribution of languages continues in first grade or whether the use of Spanish diminishes as children progress, to 40 percent in the first grade and 30 percent in the second, so that children move toward a situation where no Spanish is used at all. Such a program model differs significantly from one where the 50–50 ratio is maintained throughout all grades and both languages are maintained and developed.

Dual language instructional models have been described in a number of ways, some far more complex than others. One theorist cross-referenced the learner, the languages, the community, and the curriculum to arrive at 90 different possible kinds of programs (Mackey, 1972). A simpler typology, based on philosophical rather than linguistic factors, distinguishes between assimilationist and pluralistic program models. Assimilationist programs aim at moving ethnic minority children into the mainstream (dominant) culture. In contrast, pluralistic program models are those that support minority languages and cultures (Kjolseth, 1976).

## TRANSITIONAL BILINGUAL PROGRAMS

### Which Students Do Transitional Programs Serve?

Transitional programs serve limited English proficient (LEP) students, which for general purposes, we can define as students who have been determined to have insufficient English to function academically in an English language classroom where instruction is designed for native English speakers. Which students are actually designated as LEP may vary from state to state or even from district to district within a state, because tests and testing procedures are not uniform.

It should be noted that the labels we use are significant and shape and reflect how we respond to the world around us. *Limited English proficient* is a deficit-based term—it identifies students by what they *can't* do—and sets us up to consider serving them in a remedial or compensatory mode. As an alternative, *second language learner* is fairly neutral and lacks negative connotations, but it is also general and could include anglophone students learning a new language. Some educators, searching for a way to emphasize language-as-resource rather than language-as-problem, have begun to use terms like *potentially English proficient (PEP)* (Hamayan, 1990), and *student acquiring English (SAE)* (Escamilla, 1993). The National Board for Professional Teaching Standards, which is creating standards and assessments for advanced certification of exemplary teachers nationwide, is using the term *English as a New Language (ENL) learners* (National Board for Professional Teaching Standards, 1993).

### What Is the Goal of a Transitional Program?

The goal of transitional programs is to develop a student's proficiency in English. In a transitional program, the primary language is used for instructional support until students have reached satisfactory levels of English proficiency—usually as defined by a process involving test scores and teacher observations. Students are expected to move out of a transitional program when they are capable of functioning in an English-only classroom. In many programs, the expectation is that children will be ready to make the change after a period of approximately three years.

U.S. government policy tends to favor transitional programs—by far the most common models in use today. There are a number of problems inherent in transitional bilingual programs:

- They foster subtractive, rather than additive, bilingualism. (See Chapter 4 for a discussion of these concepts.)
- They are compensatory and do not involve the monolingual English-speaking community.
- Exit assessments may measure students' face-to-face language skills and fail to consider the specialized language skills needed for academic success. Placement in English-only classrooms on the basis of such programs can lead to academic failure. (See Chapter 6.)
- It is unrealistic to expect all children to master a second language in a three-year period.

## Transitional Programs: A Lot Better than Nothing

In 1988, the California Association for Bilingual Education published *On Course: Bilingual Education's Success in California* (Krashen & Biber), a summary and analysis of data from eight programs across the state, including transitional programs. The Eastman Avenue School in Los Angeles, a model for educators across the state, reported an increase in the California Assessment Program (CAP) scores for students who participated in a carefully structured transitional program.

On the basis of the data presented, the authors conclude (p. 17) that "properly designed bilingual programs" assist children in acquiring English and succeeding in school. Properly designed programs must provide primary language instruction in content areas, develop students' primary language literacy skills, and develop students' English skills with both dedicated English language development and content taught in English, using specially designed academic instruction. (See Chapter 7.)

## LANGUAGE MAINTENANCE PROGRAMS

Language maintenance programs are pluralistic and promote bilingualism and biliteracy for language minority students. Maintenance programs may be the most effective means of promoting English proficiency for limited English proficient students for the following reasons:

- Concepts and skills learned in a student's first language transfer to the second language.
- A strong base in a first language facilitates second language acquisition.
- Support for home language and culture builds self-esteem and enhances achievement (Hakuta & Gould, 1987).

In other words, maintenance bilingual education, which is additive rather than subtractive, leads to academic success and also facilitates the acquisition of English skills for the language minority student. (For further discussion, see Chapter 6.)

## ENRICHMENT PROGRAMS

Efforts were made in the late 1960s and early 1970s to provide dual language instructional programs for both language minority children and monolingual English children. The need, however, for language support for limited English proficient children has been overwhelming. In the face of limited resources and staffing, the response has been largely compensatory in nature. The tendency to view dual language instruction as compensatory education has eroded the political base necessary to assure services for language minority students and has denied access to bilingual education for monolingual English-speaking children as well.

Educators have begun to reconsider enrichment or two-way bilingual instruction, which provides dual language instruction for all students. Two-way programs are becoming increasingly popular in areas where magnet schools have been established to facilitate desegregation. Problems in implementing enrichment programs arise from a lack of qualified staff, constant pressure to meet the needs of increasing numbers of non-English speakers, and lack of community understanding and support for dual language instruction.

## IMMERSION PROGRAMS

Success in Canada, beginning in 1965 with the now-famous Saint-Lambert experiment, has inspired a strong interest in immersion programs. In an immersion program all the usual curricular areas are taught in a second language—this language being the medium, rather than the object, of instruction. Immersion instruction should not be confused with submersion or "sink-or-swim" instruction, where non-English-speaking children are mainstreamed in English-only classrooms without assistance and are expected to keep the pace. In an immersion classroom, the following factors apply.

- Grouping is homogeneous, and second language learners are not competing with native speakers.
- The teacher speaks the child's first language and can respond to student needs.
- Children are not expected to function immediately in their second language and can express themselves in their first.
- First language support is offered in the form of language arts instruction.
- Instruction is delivered in the second language but is carefully structured so as to maximize students' comprehension.

There are several immersion program models currently operating in the United States, as described below.

## Enrichment Immersion Programs

These programs, like the Canadian programs that inspired them, immerse monolingual English speakers in a second language. The Culver City Spanish Immersion Program in California, started in 1971, is the oldest example of a replication of the Canadian model in the United States. Enrichment immersion programs have been used as "magnets" in voluntary desegregation efforts. Such efforts expand participation in enrichment immersion programs beyond middle-class white students to working-class and black students and provide opportunities for research on the effects of immersion on speakers of nonstandard varieties of English (Genesee, 1987).

## Two-way Immersion Programs

In these innovative programs, sometimes called *developmental* or *bilingual immersion programs,* monolingual English-speaking children are immersed in a second language alongside limited English proficient children who are native speakers of the second language. English is introduced gradually until it comprises about 50 percent of the curriculum. The model is actually a combination of maintenance bilingual instruction and immersion instruction. The strength of this approach is that it aims at additive bilingualism for all the students involved.

The two-way immersion program was first implemented in San Diego, California, in 1975, and has been replicated nationwide. At River Glen Elementary School in northern California, a linguistically heterogeneous group of kindergarten children starts school each year in a classroom where Spanish is used 90 percent of the time and English 10 percent of the time. By fifth grade, English and Spanish are each used 50 percent of the time in class. The program at River Glen was started as part of a magnet school desegregation program and has been extremely successful in attracting an ethnically diverse student population. As an important outcome of the instructional program, students not only speak each other's languages, they learn to appreciate and respect each other's culture as well (Guido, 1995).

## English Immersion

Political pressure in the United States to move away from primary language instruction has resulted in experimentation with English immersion programs, sometimes called *structured immersion,* for minority students (see Table 2.1). A recently completed longitudinal study of English immersion indicates that it is less successful for minority language students than bilingual education with native language support (Ramírez et al., 1991).

## The Results of Immersion: The Canadian Experience

The implementation of carefully structured additive immersion programs may provide useful educational services to both limited English proficient and monolingual English students in the United States. Results of research and evaluation studies of French early immersion programs in Canada indicate that students:

- achieve at levels comparable to those of comparison groups who received all instruction in English
- fall behind comparison groups initially in English literacy skills but catch up to and even surpass those groups once English instruction begins

**TABLE 2.1**   Program models, goals, and outcomes

| Program Model | Goal | Outcome |
|---|---|---|
| Transitional | Proficiency in L2 for language minority students (assimilationist) | Subtractive bilingualism |
| Maintenance | Bilingualism and biliteracy for language minority students (pluralist) | Additive bilingualism |
| Enrichment/Two-way | Bilingualism and biliteracy for language minority and language majority students (pluralist) | Additive biligualism |
| Immersion | | |
| 1. Enrichment | Bilingualism and biliteracy for language majority students (pluralist) | Additive bilingualism |
| 2. Two-way | Bilingualism and biliteracy for language minority and language majority students (pluralist) | Additive bilingualism |
| 3. English immersion | Proficiency in English for language minority students (assimilationist) | Subtractive bilingualism |

Note: L1 = first language; L2 = second language. For language minority students in the United States, L2 = English.

- achieve higher levels of proficiency in the second language than students who study it as an isolated subject
- attain native-like receptive skills in their second language and, while their productive skills fall short of native proficiency, are quite capable of expressing themselves in the second language
- have heightened sensitivity to social and cultural aspects of their second culture (Cummins & Swain, 1986)

The Canadian experience with immersion instruction suggests that the model works best with children from a dominant language group who are not at risk for losing their first language since it is readily available in the environment beyond the school. In other words, immersion programs are most effective when they are linguistically and culturally additive.

## DUAL LANGUAGE INSTRUCTION IN PRIVATE SCHOOLS

Professional attention generally focuses on dual language instruction in public school settings and (despite current interest in two-way and enrichment programs) most often addresses the needs of limited English proficient children. Bilingualism, however, is widely considered the hallmark of an educated person, and dual language instruction has found outlets in the private school arena as well.

Dual language instruction for privileged sectors of society has been available in the United States for quite some time. For example, Bryn Mawr School in Baltimore, Maryland, established in 1885, offers French, Latin, Greek, German, and Spanish as enrichment for students in kindergarten through fifth grade (Tomlinson & Eastwick, 1980).

According to one comprehensive report, there are approximately 6,500 private schools in the United States that provide some form of education in a language other than English. The Jewish community accounts for nearly half that number, providing schooling in both Hebrew and Yiddish. But at least 108 languages are represented in private schools (Fishman, 1985).

As part of a federal project on bilingual education, researchers made site visits to 24 private schools with dual language instructional programs. They found that private schools use many of the same methods as public schools for providing dual language instruction. Despite the lack of innovation, private dual language programs are distinguished by their emphasis on the value of knowing two languages (Elford & Woodford, 1982).

Reports in the popular press indicate that demand for second language instruction has spread to include private preschools (Wells, 1986). The value placed on bilingualism by those who can afford to pay for private schooling raises an important issue: Why is dual language instruction desirable for a socioeconomic elite but undesirable for minority language groups? Perhaps experimental two-way enrichment programs will change attitudes about bilingualism and dual language instruction.

## BILINGUAL TEACHERS

### What Competencies Do Bilingual Teachers Have?

All too often, lay people and even some professionals assume that bilingual teachers are teachers who speak two languages. That would be the same as assuming that an English teacher is any person who speaks, reads, and writes English! A good bilingual teacher, like any good teacher, has attitudes, knowledge, and skills that are particular to the students and the subject matter. What good teachers do and what they need to know to do it are subjects of ongoing conversation among professionals at every level.

Clearly, bilingual teachers need to be bilingual and biliterate in English and their students' language. They also need to understand the nature of language and how languages are learned so they can create appropriate learning environments for second language learners.

In addition, they must understand their students' culture in ways that transcend surface culture, and address the values and beliefs that underlie the ways their students act in and out of classrooms. Understanding culture, combined with awareness of the social contexts of their students, allow effective bilingual teachers to reach out and connect with the families and communities of the students they serve. Understanding the historical and political contexts of bilingual education and of their students supports teachers' abilities to advocate for their students' needs in a climate increasingly characterized by hostility towards newcomers and diversity.

Finally, like all teachers, bilingual teachers must be skilled at assessing students' needs, planning appropriate goals, objectives, and activities to meet those needs, and gathering evaluative data on an ongoing basis as students grow and change. Bilingual teachers plan and prepare in more than one language, and strive to meet multiple content and language objectives as students learn in two languages and through two languages.

### Bilingual and English as a Second Language Teachers

There is increasing understanding in the field that bilingual teachers and English as a second language (ESL) teachers—sometimes called *English language development (ELD)* teachers—serve the same students, work toward the same objectives, and in many respects bring the same competencies to the endeavor. As a result recognizing the overlap between the tasks and preparation of both bilingual and ESL teachers, California recently created a new credential configuration called the *Bilingual Crosscultural Language Academic Development/ Crosscultural Language Academic Development (BCLAD/CLAD)* emphasis.

Both BCLAD and CLAD teachers are expected to have knowledge of the structure of language and the processes of first language learning and second language development. In addition, they should understand the nature of culture and the dynamics of cultures in contact and cultures in conflict. They are expected to understand the nature and dynamics of bilingual instructional models and methods, since it is assumed that BCLAD and CLAD teachers will work cooperatively to meet the needs of second language learners. Both CLAD and BCLAD teachers are prepared and authorized to deliver instruction in ESL and in content, using English as the medium of instruction.

BCLAD teachers, in addition, have proficiency in and can deliver instruction in the students' primary language and demonstrate in-depth knowledge of the culture of the students they serve. The California model is intended to unify the training of teachers who serve limited English proficient students and may serve as a model for other states in the future.

## THE ROLE OF PARAPROFESSIONALS

In general, the instructional role of a paraprofessional is restricted to review and follow-up instruction or to monitoring and assisting students who have received direct instruction from a teacher. In many situations, however, the paraprofessional is the only adult in a classroom who speaks the language of a particular student or group of students. In such cases, the paraprofessional may be called on to plan and deliver instruction. In addition, a teacher may call on a paraprofessional to assist in communicating with a language minority student's parents, either in writing or in person.

Because paraprofessionals who work with language minority and limited English proficient students may have to take on responsibilities generally reserved to the teacher in charge, they should receive training related to the language and culture of their students, language development, and dual language instructional approaches and methods.

In addition, bilingual teachers need to develop an understanding of ways to effectively work with and develop the skills of paraprofessionals, community liaisons, and parent volunteers, so as to maximize the support they receive in their classrooms.

## BILINGUAL EDUCATION AND MULTICULTURAL EDUCATION

In practice, educators often refer to bilingual/multicultural education. Because the terms appear side by side, bilingual and multicultural education are erroneously construed as identical. In theory, the two are not one and the same thing, although there is a relationship between dual language instruction and multi-cultural education.

## What Is Multicultural Education?

Carlos Cortés, a leading exponent of multicultural education, begins his definition by describing what multicultural education is *not* (1990). He asserts that multicultural education is not the celebration of holidays or the inclusion of special history days or weeks in the curriculum—an approach that James Banks, another important multicultural theorist, refers to as "tepees and chitlins" and "heroes and holidays" (1977). Banks calls such approaches to multicultural education *additive*—they tack on bits and pieces to the existing curriculum, but they do not alter the basic structure of schooling. Cortés and Banks also agree that multicultural education is not the study of a particular ethnic group, although ethnic studies may contribute to multicultural education by generating the scholarship necessary to build an inclusive curriculum. Finally, multicultural education is not a compensatory program for students who are identified as "minority."

Multicultural education, in its broadest sense, entails educational reform or restructuring to empower students, provide all students with equitable opportunities, and enable all students to function comfortably and effectively in a pluralist democracy (Cortés, 1990; Nieto, 1992). Current theorists favor a social reconstructionist multicultural approach. Social reconstructionists work toward empowering students to actively engage their own life circumstances and alter them in the direction of social equity and justice. This point of view is rooted in the educational philosophy of critical pedagogy.

Critical pedagogy rejects what Paolo Freire (1970) has termed the *banking* concept of education, where teachers make deposits of knowledge into their students—a system which assumes that teachers are experts and students are not. In critical pedagogy, students are encouraged to pose their own questions and seek their own answers. Critical pedagogy assumes that students are inquisitive and creative and can use themselves and their environments as sources for both problems and their solutions.

Critical approaches underlie programs such as *Como Ellos Lo Ven* (Lessow-Hurley, 1977). In that project, students from migrant farmwork families in Longmont, Colorado, created a documentary of their lives, using their own photographs and narratives based on those images to produce a book which was then incorporated into the reading program in their class.

In another project based in critical pedagogy, Flor Ada engaged Spanish-speaking parents in the Pajaro Valley in California in developing their children's literacy skills (Flor Ada, 1988). Through presentations and small-group discussions, parents were introduced to Spanish language children's literature and to ways of encouraging their children to read and write. As a result of their participation, parents came to understand the value of their home language, to see themselves as essential participants in their children's education, and to develop their own critical literacy skills as a key to understanding their world.

Multicultural education, broadly conceived, touches every aspect of school life—from the books and materials students use to the distribution of power within the school community. Nieto (1992) asserts that multicultural education is basic and pervasive. Cortés sums up his definition of multicultural education as "a continuous, integrated, multiethnic, multidisciplinary process for educating all American students about diversity, a curricular basic oriented toward preparing young people to live with pride and understanding in our multiethnic present and increasingly multiethnic future" (p. 3).

In its fullest sense, multicultural education is not a program that is implemented on Monday or in January, but a total rethinking of the way we do schooling in a diverse society with a democratic civic framework.

## What Is the Connection between Bilingual Education and Multicultural Education?

In the professional arena, bilingual and multicultural education have developed separately, with separate journals, professional associations, and constituencies. Bilingual education is often erroneously construed as compensatory education for speakers of minority languages, while multicultural education is often mistakenly conceptualized as a program for African American students. We have seen that both bilingual and multicultural education admit to much more inclusive and useful definitions than those with a compensatory or deficit focus. What then is the connection between these two concepts?

Both multicultural and bilingual education subscribe to the fundamental idea that schooling should utilize students' knowledge of the world as a starting point and resource for learning. For all students, language is perhaps the single most important aspect of culture since language is the primary means by which each of us is enculturated—that is, brought into our particular communities of behavior and belief. For language minority students, primary language is a deep resource which schooling should validate and enhance. Using the students' first language is empowering since it validates students' culture. It is equitable to the extent that it provides equal access to the curriculum. And when it develops and maintains students' primary language alongside English, it enhances their preparation to function in an increasingly pluralist environment. In other words, bilingual education that values and promotes bilingualism and biliteracy is multicultural as well.

Bilingualism is an asset in an increasingly multicultural society and a global economy. English-only students benefit from an education that allows them to learn, and learn in more than one language, and prepares them to function effectively in a world characterized by diversity. When we provide a bilingual education to all students, we meet many of the goals embodied in broad definitions of multicultural education. In sum, while bilingual and multicultural education are not necessarily identical, all students can benefit from an education that is bilingual and multicultural.

## SUMMARY

Dual language instruction may be transitional or maintenance-oriented. Immersion models have received attention recently because they have proven effective in Canada for teaching minority languages to majority children. A variety of immersion designs are currently being tried in the United States. Enrichment programs that provide second language instruction for monolingual English speakers are increasing in popularity. Dual language programs are available in private schools as well.

Teachers who work in dual language instructional settings need specialized training in both bilingual and multicultural education, as do the paraprofessionals that assist them. Bilingual and multicultural education are not identical, but many basic dispositions, concepts, and skills are common to both fields, and student empowerment is a key concept in both.

## ACTIVITIES AND QUESTIONS TO THINK ABOUT

1. Visit a public, dual language instructional program. Interview a program administrator, a teacher, a parent, and a student enrolled in the program. Find out what they perceive the goals of the program to be. Analyze the program design. Does the program model fit the goals that the participants envision?

2. Visit a private school that offers dual language instruction. What program model is in use? What are the goals of administrators, teachers, parents, and students in this school? Describe the student population of the school.

3. Visit a public school and analyze the curriculum from a multicultural perspective. Consider curriculum in its broadest sense: look at the physical plant, the way instruction is organized, the makeup of the staff and the distribution of authority, and the materials on display and in use for instruction. To what extent does the school reach for the broadest goals of multicultural education?

## SUGGESTIONS FOR FURTHER READING

Cummins, J. (1989). *Empowering minority students.* Sacramento: California Association for Bilingual Education.

This book examines the relationship between minority students' experience of schooling and the sociopolitical context of education. Language and bilingual education are explored from the perspective of critical pedagogy, and programs that have been successful for language minority students are described.

Cummins, J., & Swain, M. (1986). *Bilingualism in education.* London: Longman.

This book explores the nature of bilingual proficiency and suggests that positive linguistic, cognitive, and academic consequences result from high levels of proficiency in two languages. Results of research and evaluation studies related to Canadian French immersion programs are described in detail.

Genesee, F. (1987). *Learning through two languages: Studies of immersion and bilingual education.* Rowley, MA: Newbury House.
This book examines immersion programs for majority students in Canada and bilingual programs for minority language students in the United States. A chapter on immersion in the United States details programs in California, Maryland, and Ohio.

Genesee, F. (Ed.). (1994). *Educating second language children: The whole child, the whole curriculum, the whole community.* Cambridge, England: The Cambridge University Press.
This collection of articles links schools, families, and communities, and addresses the second language learner's experience in all those contexts, reaching beyond language to incorporate social and cultural dimensions as well.

Krashen, S., & Biber, D. (1988). *On course: Bilingual education's success in California.* Sacramento: California Association for Bilingual Education.
Following a summary of a rationale for primary language instruction, this book provides descriptions of bilingual programs in California that have been successful in improving student achievement.

Nieto, S. (1992). *Affirming diversity: The sociopolitical context of multicultural education.* White Plains, NY: Longman.
An excellent overview of the many issues and themes related to multicultural education, this book is particularly engaging because it includes transcripts of interviews with students. The author analyzes the salient themes expressed by the students. The students' voices lend authenticity to the issues, and the analyses are relevant and thought provoking.

Office of Bilingual Bicultural Education, California State Department of Education. (1984). *Studies on immersion education: A collection for United States educators.* Sacramento: California State Department of Education.
The first section of this book presents an overview of major issues related to immersion programs. The second section includes descriptions of programs in Canada. Section 3 looks at immersion education in the United States.

Olsen, L., et al. (1994). *The unfinished journey: Restructuring schools in a diverse society.* San Francisco: California Tomorrow.
Using descriptions of a number of programs currently in place, this report shows how schools can restructure effectively to meet the needs of diverse student populations.

Ramírez, A. J. (1985). *Bilingualism through schooling: Cross-cultural education for minority and majority students.* Albany: State University of New York Press.
An overview of issues and topics related to dual language instruction for all students, this book contains a section devoted to bilingual program models. Various typologies are reviewed within the framework of language policy.

Skutnabb-Kangas, T. (1981). *Bilingualism or not: The education of minorities.* Clevedon, Avon (England): Multilingual Matters.
Far more than a simple discussion of program models, this book provides an insightful analysis of bilingualism and the education of minorities from a broad political perspective. Included are discussions of bilingualism of children from a variety of language backgrounds, the neurolinguistic and cognitive aspects of bilingualism, the impact of social and educational policy on immigrant children, and a typology of dual language programs accounting for differences between majority and minority students.

# chapter 3

# Aspects of Language

In this chapter you are asked to think critically about the nature of language. This may be difficult because language is almost invisible to us. We acquire language when we are very young and use it for a multitude of purposes every day. But unless we have a scholarly interest, we rarely stop to look at it.

Textbooks on linguistics or communication disorders provide detailed introductions to the concept of language. This chapter will not investigate language in depth but is intended as an overview of various technical and academic ways of looking at language.

From a teacher's point of view, it is important to know what language is and how it works, because language should be used in a planned way—much as we use other instructional materials and media. This chapter has two purposes, which will allow us to objectify language so that we can use it effectively for dual language instruction. First, we will define language and look at its component parts. By defining language, we will render it more visible and acquire the basic vocabulary necessary to discuss numerous aspects of dual language instruction.

Second, we will consider some of the common preconceived notions about language. We have strong emotional bonds to our language because it is the vehicle through which we convey our experience and culture. Therefore, we need to separate basic concepts about language from attitudes that may interfere with our ability to use language as a classroom tool or to deal equitably with children whose language backgrounds differ from our own.

## THE STUDY OF LANGUAGE

The study of dual language instruction requires us to consider language from at least three different perspectives. *Linguistics* describes the structural aspects of language. Much of the basic vocabulary needed to discuss language acquisition and language proficiency comes from the field of linguistics.

*Psycholinguistics* deals with the relationship of language and the mind. Psycholinguists consider how language is acquired and how language is processed in the human mind.

*Sociolinguistics* is the relatively new and exciting field of inquiry that investigates how language works in society. Sociolinguists study the language dynamics of everyday interactions between people. If you have ever considered dialect differences or the manner in which people alter their speech when addressing a superior or a member of the opposite sex, you have made sociolinguistic observations.

Planning and delivery of effective dual language instruction are based on theory, research, and practical applications from all these areas of language inquiry.

## WHAT IS LANGUAGE?

The American Speech-Language-Hearing Association defines *language* as a complex and dynamic system of conventional symbols used in various modes for communication and thought (American Speech-Language-Hearing Association, 1983). Let us take a closer look at this definition.

A system is organized, governed by rules, and works toward a purpose. Automobile engines and the digestive tract are examples of systems. Language is a system—it is ordered and purposeful. The essential purpose of language is communication. A careful focus on the purpose of language dispels many unfortunate attitudes people have about languages and, concomitantly, about each other. Also, as we shall see, understanding the basic purpose of language is useful for understanding how we acquire languages and provides important insights as to how we should teach languages.

Language is an orderly combination of conventional symbols. The symbols are the words we use to label the objects, actions, and ideas that we perceive in our reality. These symbols are conventional—that is, we assign a socially agreed upon symbol to objects and ideas so we can talk about them. We all agree on a name for a particular object or idea for purposes of communication.

In English, for example, we use *chair* to identify a common object used for supporting us in a sitting posture. A Spanish speaker refers to the same object as *silla*. It's altogether arbitrary: no matter what you call it, you can still sit on it. The concept of the arbitrary nature of symbols used in language becomes important when we start to investigate bilingualism. As we shall see, bilingual people have a strong understanding of the arbitrary nature of the symbols of language, which enhances their problem-solving skills.

## SUBSYSTEMS OF LANGUAGE

Breaking language down into its subsystems facilitates understanding how it works and provides us with some of the vocabulary necessary for discussing language acquisition, language proficiency, and second language instruction. Language is generally considered to have five fundamental subsystems, which are described below.

### The Phonological System

The phonological system is the sound system of a language. When we hear speech, we perceive phonemes, the smallest distinguishable units of sound that carry meaning for us in our language.

It might seem as though we ought to be able to hear the distinctions between all the sounds that humans produce, but that is not the case. Each language makes use of only a small number of the wide range of possible sounds that human beings are capable of uttering and discerning.

For example, in English it makes a significant difference to you if someone *pats* you on the head or *bats* you on the head. But in some languages, the sounds that we write as *p* and *b* are heard as identical, a phenomenon easier to understand if you consider that both sounds are produced using the same parts of the mouth in the same fashion. The only difference is that the initial sound in *bat* includes the use of voicing, while the initial sound in *pat* does not. Not all languages distinguish between voiced and voiceless sounds, which sound distinctive to native English speakers. For speakers of languages that do not distinguish between these sounds, English words such as *ban* and *pan* or *bay* and *pay* sound alike.

Sign languages, not having sound systems, have an equivalent system known as *cherology*. Cheremes are the smallest units of gesture that are distinguishable and carry meaning to a speaker of sign (Wilbur, 1980).

### The Morphological System

The morphological system is the system of how words are built. Morphemes are meaningful units, which can sometimes stand alone as words, but often appear in combination with other morphemes. For example, the word *girl* has one morpheme, which carries the meaning of a young female human. *Girls* has two morphemes. The second morpheme, *-s*, indicates the concept of plural. *Girls* is a single example, which sidesteps more complicated morphological issues, such as the relationship between *man* and *men*. A complex analysis of the theory of morphology is out of place here. It is important to know that words are built systematically, much as sentences are.

## Syntax

*Syntax* refers to the structure or architecture of sentences. It is common but inaccurate to think of syntax as grammar. Syntax, however, is descriptive rather than prescriptive. For example, "I don't have a pencil" is recognizable to a native speaker of English as an acceptable sentence. On the other hand, "A pencil don't have I" sounds awkward. It does not conform to the generally accepted patterns or rules of English.

On the other hand, look at the sentence "I ain't got no pencil." A native speaker of American English knows that it is an English sentence and conforms to English syntax. Nevertheless, we have a tendency to judge "I ain't got no pencil" as incorrect English. It is not standard usage, and its use would be ill-advised for a formal situation such as an employment interview. From a purely descriptive standpoint, however, it fits into basic English sentence patterns. Despite the fact that it may make schoolteachers shudder, it is used in classrooms countless times every day, and, from a syntactical point of view, it works in English.

In sum, *syntax* refers to the rules that govern a language. *Grammar*, on the other hand, has a prescriptive connotation—it looks at whether or not a particular construction conforms to a language standard. We shall analyze the meaning of standard language later in this chapter.

## Semantics

*Semantics* is the study of meaning. Semantics was considered the purview of philosophers until fairly recently. Modern analyses have led linguists to conclude that while meaning and structure are inextricably connected, syntactical analysis of language is insufficient to explain meaning (Hayes, Ornstein, & Gage, 1977). One area of inquiry in semantics is the study of words. Words can be analyzed with reference to their denotations. Earlier in this chapter, we talked about conventional symbols, and we agreed that *chair* refers to a piece of furniture used for sitting. *Chair*, however, can denote several things, depending on the context. In a committee meeting, for example, *chair* may well denote the person who organizes the meeting or the action of leading the group.

Words also have connotations that supplement their denotations. While the words *Asian* and *rice-eater* may refer to the same individual, they have very different connotations. *Asian* refers to a person's geographical or cultural origins; *rice-eater* has pejorative connotations far beyond an observation on dietary habits.

Semantics also studies phrases and sentences and analyzes different kinds of ambiguities. For example, the sentence "They were hunting dogs" has structural ambiguities. Thus, two differing meanings are represented with the same surface structure of language. As language users, we daily sort out many different and ambiguous meanings. Our intuitive understanding of semantics enables us to sort out correct meanings by relying on linguistic context.

## Pragmatics

Pragmatics is not an internal linguistic subsystem, such as phonology, morphology, syntax, and semantics. Rather it is the system of the use of language in social contexts. Language use is determined by the function of an interaction and by the relationship of the people involved (Bloom & Lahey, 1978). For example, "I now pronounce you man and wife" has no meaning if uttered by a child in play but significant consequences when stated by an appropriate official during a wedding ceremony.

In language, one form may serve several functions. "It's ten after five" may be a response to a direct question. It may also be a way of suggesting to people that they have arrived behind schedule. Uttered in a particular context, it may mean "We're going to get stuck in rush-hour traffic!" Conversely, one function may take many forms. The question "Can we begin?" and the hint "We're running short on time" both serve the same function.

Native speakers intuitively understand pragmatic systems. If someone asks, "Can you tell me the time?" a native English speaker, acting on knowledge about language and social context, knows that it is inappropriate to answer yes.

## OTHER ASPECTS OF COMMUNICATION

Apart from language, communication is enhanced by paralinguistic ("beyond language") and nonlinguistic messages, which can be transmitted in conjunction with language or without the aid of language. Paralinguistic mechanisms include intonation, stress, rate of speech, and pauses or hesitations. Nonlinguistic behaviors include gestures, facial expressions, and body language, among others.

Paralinguistic and nonlinguistic behaviors differ from culture to culture and language to language. Such differences are often the cause of misunderstandings in cross-cultural situations. Students who wish to become proficient in a second language should pay careful attention to the nonverbal behaviors that pertain to the languages they are studying.

## LANGUAGE ATTITUDES

In the introduction to this chapter, we said that it is necessary to identify the attitudes or biases we have and separate them from basic concepts about language. This is necessary so that we can use language as an instructional tool and also respond equitably to students with a language background different from our own.

It is difficult to pinpoint attitudes we hold about language, because the emotional bond we have to our native language is extremely strong. Soren Kierkegaard, the nineteenth-century Danish philosopher and writer, once referred to the porridge his mother prepared for him when he was a child. It seemed, he reflected, as though no other porridge could ever be as flavorful. We can draw an analogy between language and Kierkegaard's porridge—no language ever seems quite as rich or evocative as our own.

In this section we will investigate a few of the commonly held attitudes about language.

## Are Some Languages Better than Others?

One prevalent attitude is that some languages or varieties of a language are more correct or better than others. For example, Spanish speakers are often asked if they speak Castilian. The Spanish word for Castilian is *castellano*. In Spain *castellano* refers to the regional dialect of the province of Castile. In parts of Latin America, *castellano* is used to refer to Spanish in general. The uninformed English speaker, however, who refers to Castilian generally means something along the lines of "the King's English"—a proper, high-class form of the language.

This attitude and many others can be dispelled by focusing on the fact that the primary purpose of language is communication. A Spanish speaker answering the phone in Argentina says *allo* (hello). Other Latin Americans pick up the receiver and say *diga* (speak). Mexicans say *bueno* (good or well). Mexicans joke about the expression, claiming that their phone system is so bad that anytime they can get a call through is *bueno!* None of these responses is better than any other. Depending on where you are, there are many appropriate ways to answer a phone in Spanish. It makes sense to facilitate communication by responding according to local custom.

## Are Some Languages More Expressive than Others?

One common attitude that people hold about language is that there are ideas or feelings that can be expressed in one language that can't be expressed in another. An expression of this bias is that some languages are less logical than others. In particular, people sometimes suggest that some languages are not useful for communicating about technology.

As Muriel Saville-Troike (1982) remarks, "While all languages may be inherently capable of serving all purposes humans may ask of them, specific languages evolve differentially through processes of variation, adaptation, and selection" (p. 82). In other words, as people in a society have a need to communicate in a particular way or about a particular subject, their language expands and adapts to meet their need.

For example, there are several cultures in the South Pacific that commonly use a large squashlike vegetable we call *breadfruit* for a variety of purposes. Breadfruit is used as a basic food, but also serves several ritual and ceremonial purposes. People in those cultures have many words for breadfruit that indicate its color, ripeness, size, and particular use. In the United States we rarely encounter a breadfruit, and the one name we have for it may not be familiar to you at all. Nevertheless, with some circumlocution and explanation, English can produce all the nuances necessary to talk about breadfruit.

Some languages borrow to meet expanding technological needs. There is a bias against borrowing, and some governments have even passed laws to limit loan words. According to an article in *Newsweek* (Doerner, 1987), the French government has established a secretary of state for Francophone affairs, and judgments have been levied against companies that use English words in advertising in lieu of French equivalents.

Hebrew, however, is an example of a language that has borrowed extensively to meet the needs of modernization and yet has maintained its linguistic integrity. Preserved for centuries almost exclusively as a liturgical language, Hebrew came into everyday use with the creation of the state of Israel in 1948. Biblical Hebrew was, of course, incompatible with the demands of the modern world. It might be possible, for example, to create a circumlocution for *telephone* by saying "a way to talk to people at a distance through wires." But that would be cumbersome in real-life situations when you want to say, "Answer the telephone!" So Hebrew borrowed the word *telephone,* and in Hebrew it sounds much like the English word.

We have looked at only a few of the many possible attitudes about language. Linguists agree that all languages are linguistically equal and that every language is equally capable of expressing whatever its speakers need to communicate. Attitudes about language persist, however, because people feel a close emotional tie to the language they speak. Such attitudes are misinterpretations of the nature and purpose of language as a human endeavor.

## LANGUAGE VARIETIES

### Standard

The term *standard* has been used in the foregoing section, but it has not been defined. It is commonly assumed that there is a standard, fixed, and correct form of a language against which we can measure a given sample of that language. But the concept of an immutable and proper language form contradicts the very nature of language itself. As we have seen, language is flexible and responsive, and changes constantly to meet the communication needs of its speakers.

Students of language sometimes suggest that a language is a dialect with an army. That somewhat humorous assertion gets close to the truth about language variation. The term *standard* is elusive precisely because it has its roots in politics rather than in any basic truth about language.

Standard language is the language of the group in power. Formal attempts are made to standardize language. For example, Spanish is regulated by 22 language academies, the oldest of which is the *Real Academia Española* (the Royal Spanish Academy), created in Spain in 1713 by King Philip V.

The most recent academy was established in New York in 1987 in an attempt to protect Spanish from becoming anglicized (Chavez, 1987). The United States has the fifth-largest Spanish-speaking population in the world, and Spanish is in constant contact with English. One result is words like *carpeta* (rug), *roofo* (roof), and *lonche* (lunch). Another outcome is the addition of words like *taco* and *burrito* to the American English lexicon.

Spanish, along with the other Romance languages, is itself the product of languages in contact. When the Romans conquered Iberia, speakers of indigenous Iberian languages learned Latin. They spoke it with an accent, overlaid grammatical structures from their native tongues, and sprinkled it with local words for familiar concepts and objects. That natural process formed the basis for what we know as modern Spanish.

Languages are dynamic; they change to meet the communication needs of their speakers. It is possible for a "language government" such as an academy to set a standard. The question, however, is not so much what is the standard as who is doing the setting.

## Dialect

Dialects are variations of a language used by particular groups of people. Regional dialects often have distinct vocabularies. A water pistol on the East coast of the United States is a squirt gun on the West Coast. In Spanish, a peach is *melocotón* in Puerto Rico and a *durazno* in Mexico. Languages may also differ phonologically or syntactically from place to place.

Regional differences in languages may reflect differences in language history. American English includes usages that sound archaic to the British ear and may well be remnants from Colonial times. American English also includes a large lexicon of words borrowed from Spanish (McCrum, Cran, & MacNeil, 1986).

People often relate regional dialects to stereotypes. For example, in the United States, speakers of Bostonian dialects are sometimes considered "stuffy." Southerners are said to drawl and are considered lazy and slow moving. Such biases have nothing to do with the real nature of dialects or the people who speak them. Despite our biases, regional differences present few problems for native speakers. Humans are quite responsive to language and quite flexible in their ability to communicate.

Much as language varies from place to place, it also varies among different social groups. Social variations of language are sometimes called *sociolects.* Professor Higgins, in *My Fair Lady,* was well aware of the differing responses people have to different sociolects when he undertook his project of turning a flower seller into a member of high society.

Any individual's particular speech, or *idiolect,* is influenced by both regional and social class factors. From a teacher's viewpoint, it is important to remember that language can vary for many reasons and to be conscious of the biases that may come into play when we are exposed to different varieties of language. This awareness will help us avoid prejudging a student's abilities based on our own perceptions of language.

## Register

People use different varieties of language, depending on the setting, their relationship to the person to whom they are speaking, and the function of the interaction. A *register* is a situationally appropriate form of a language.

Sociolinguistic concepts such as register are important to consider when assessing language proficiency and providing second language instruction. A person learning a second language may have a good accent or control of syntax and still lack the ability to function in a variety of life situations. You have experienced that, for example, if you learned a second language in a classroom setting and then attempted to enter into the quick give-and-take of an informal gathering among friends.

## But Is It Slang?

The word *slang* is commonly used to refer, somewhat pejoratively, to nonstandard speech. Speakers of one variety of English, for example, may comment that speakers of another variety "speak slang." From a professional perspective, *slang* has a more precise meaning. According to one linguist, "One of the main defining features of 'slang' appears to be its ephemeral nature (Wardhaugh, 1993, p. 165)." In other words, slang is usage that is popular for a while and then fades away. In some cases, however, slang may become acceptable and enter common usage. In that case, it is no longer slang.

## SUMMARY

Language is a system of arbitrary symbols used for communication. The field of linguistics describes the structure of language. Psycholinguistics investigates the relationship of language to the human mind, while sociolinguistics investigates how language varies as it is used in social situations. People have unfounded and emotional biases about language, but, in fact, all languages are responsive to the communication needs of their speakers and are equally suited for communication. Standards are arbitrary and determined by the dominant group in any society. Understanding the nature of language and objectifying it as a tool are essential to dual language instruction.

## ACTIVITIES AND QUESTIONS TO THINK ABOUT

1. Read and analyze the following verse from the poem "Jabberwocky" by Lewis Carroll: What language is it written in? How do you know? What information does each subsystem of language give you for making that determination?

> 'Twas brillig and the slithy toves
> Did gyre and gimble in the wabe:
> All mimsy were the borogoves,
> And the mome raths outgrabe.

2. Identify the ambiguity in each of the following sentences and add words, a phrase, or a sentence to eliminate it.

> John married Isabel.
>
> The American history teacher is good looking.
>
> Martha thinks she is a genius.

3. Read the following letter, which appeared in the *New York Times.* Analyze the author's language attitudes. Does the author's beliefs about language match up with the understandings you have about the nature of language?

> *To the Editor:*
> *As a native of Japan, I am well aware of the importance of the Confucian ethic as an explanation for the academic success of Asian students. However, there may exist another reason why Japanese children, say at Sendai, can do better in mathematics. When I was tutoring my wife's granddaughter, who is a Caucasian, I was struck by the awkwardness of the English language for reciting the multiplication table.*
> *As an example, you must pronounce 4 × 4 = 16 as "4 times 4 is 16" in a rather unrhythmical way. We can say the same in Japanese, "shi-shi-ju-roku" with a singsong musical rhythm. We learn the multiplication table up to 10 × 10 in this fashion. Even after 39 years in this country, I revert to the Japanese method because of its ease.*
> *I can well imagine that the relative difficulty of memorizing the multiplication table in English may cause boredom and loss of interest in math for many youngsters in this country. Of course, math does not consist solely of such routine. However, this example demonstrates the subtle influence of language structure.*
> *Another possibility is the effect of the tone of the language. Japanese is rather imprecise but psychologically warmer than the more precise but perhaps drier character of the English language. This subtle difference may also cause different psychological attitudes in the learning process of youngsters.*

4. A letter appeared in an advice column in a magazine aimed at young women. The letter writer commented that she would prefer to be called a *girl* or a *lady* than a *woman,* concluding "Women must battle patriarchy, but we must choose our battles." The response from the columnist suggested, "Ponder the following headlines:

> Women Battle Patriarchy;
>
> Ladies Battle Patriarchy;
>
> Girls Battle Patriarchy." (Goldhor Lerner, 1993, p. 40).

Do these three headlines sound different to you? Why? What subsystem are you working with when you try to answer these questions?

5. Working with your classmates, try to translate the following British sentences into American English:

> My car needs work on the buffer, the windscreen, the bonnet, and the wings.
> On the way home could you stop at the chemist's and the news agent?
> Take the lift. It's just past the pillar box.
> I called the booking office, and they were out of stalls.
> Run those through the franking machine and post them.

6. Which of the following assertions are true? Why or why not?

> Italian is more romantic than English.
> Physics and mathematics cannot be discussed in Navajo.
> English is the most logical language in the world.
> Languages that have writing systems are more creative than languages that do not.
> The languages of primitive societies do not have complex syntactical systems.
> "He gots a hat" is not English.

7. According to an article in the *New York Times* ("Speech Therapist," 1993), there is a speech therapist in New York who specializes in transforming people's accents. According to the article "He teaches senators how to drop their regional accents when they are in Washington, and how to pick them up again on the campaign trail" (p. A10). Why would a public figure want to be able to change language varieties at will?

8. Slang is a form of language that is popular for a short period of time. In some cases, slang enters the language mainstream and may become standard usage. The word *dis,* derived from disrespect, originated among African American young people, gained popularity among young people in general, and is now appearing frequently in newspapers and magazines. Can you think of any other examples of slang that have moved toward the linguistic mainstream?

9. Jargon is specialized occupational related language. Think about your own employment. What kinds of specialized language do you use?


## SUGGESTIONS FOR FURTHER READING

Bryson, B. (1994). *Made in America: An informal history of the English language in the United States.* New York: William Morrow.
   You might be surpised to know that President Benjamin Harrison established a Board on Geographic Names in an attempt to standardize place naming in the United States. According to this entertaining book, Greasy Corner, Arkansas, and Bugtussle, Texas, among others equally picturesque, are still on the map. *Made in America* is a treat for language students.

Chaika, E. (1989). *Language: The social mirror* (2nd ed.). Rowley, MA: Newbury House.
A comprehensive introduction to sociolinguistics, this book includes discussion of dialects, sociolects, and styles, as well as analysis of nonverbal behaviors and their role in communication. Lively examples and reference to up-to-date issues, such as the difference between the languages of women and men, make this a particularly readable resource.

Crystal, D. (1987). *The Cambridge encyclopedia of language.* Cambridge, Eng.: Cambridge University Press.
This book has 65 sections, each of which addresses a major theme in language study and manages to touch on everything you ever wanted to know about language in an entertaining format that includes maps, illustrations, and lists of every description.

Morris, D. (1977). *Manwatching: A field guide to human behavior.* New York: Harry N. Abrams.
An entertaining analysis of nonlinguistic communication, this colorfully illustrated book includes discussion of gestures, eye contact, clothing, cosmetics, use of objects, and other human behaviors that transmit messages.

Nobel, B. L. (1982). *Linguistics for bilinguals.* Rowley, MA: Newbury House.
An introduction to basic linguistics, this book includes a valuable discussion of language attitudes. Spanish-English bilinguals will enjoy this book, which uses Spanish for many of its illustrations.

Saville-Troike, M. (1982). *The ethnography of communication: An introduction.* Oxford: Basil Blackwell.
A discussion of culturally constituted patterns of communication and methods for describing them, this book includes a discussion of basic sociolinguistic terms and language varieties, enlivened by examples from many different languages and cultures.

Tannen, D. (1990). *You just don't understand: Women and men in conversation.* New York: Morrow.
Gender differences are fascinating, and it's not surprising that this discussion of the ways that men and women use language was a long-standing bestseller.

Wardhaugh, R. (1993). *Investigating language: Central problems in linguistics.* Oxford: Basil Blackwell.
An excellent overview of language and the theories about how humans learn it. Includes a glossary of basic terms.

# chapter 4

# Language Development

In the period between birth and the age of four or five, children learn to express themselves quite completely with language. How they accomplish this impressive feat is not completely understood, although great strides have been made in the study of language development in the last 25 years.

A survey of the research in language development is a enormous undertaking. An understanding, however, of how children acquire language is essential for dual language curriculum development and instruction. This chapter will present a brief overview of first language development and second language acquisition theories.

## FIRST LANGUAGE DEVELOPMENT: MEMORIZING OR HYPOTHESIZING?

People often assume that children develop a first language by simply imitating what they hear around them; in fact, that was once the traditional view of first language development. According to the behaviorist view, for example, children reproduce language or approximate imitations of what they hear and are reinforced by rewards such as attention or response.

While such views were held widely well into the twentieth century, the notion that imitation and habit formation are the primary bases for language development is flawed. Imitation theory does not account for the creative capacity of language—the child's ability to produce original utterances.

The well-known linguist Noam Chomsky revolutionized thinking about language development in the early 1950s when he suggested that children are born with an innate capacity to develop language. Chomsky suggested that children have a built-in mechanism, which he called the *Language Acquisition Device,* or *LAD,* which preprograms them to develop grammar based on the linguistic input they receive. Today it's easy to create an analogy for Chomsky's model based on computers: think of the LAD as the operating system and a particular language as software, installed as input is received.

Chomsky's view dramatically altered thinking about language development. Psycholinguists moved away from the traditional behaviorist idea that language is developed through habit formation and began to consider the idea that children discover the organizing principles of the language they are exposed to. Recent theory has expanded Chomsky's original focus on syntax, suggesting that children make sense of semantic and pragmatic systems of language as well. Overall, however, modern theories agree that children develop language by hypothesis testing, or rule finding.

## Rule Finding

As we saw in the first chapter, language is a system, governed by rules at the phonological, morphological, syntactical, semantic, and pragmatic levels. The rule-finding approach to language development suggests that children develop hypotheses about the rules of their language based on the input they receive and then test those hypotheses by trying them out.

The evidence we have for children's rule finding comes from the "errors" they make when they apply the rules they have formulated. *Error* has a special meaning in this context. It does not mean *mistake,* but refers instead to the forms generated by applying rules that do not take irregularities or exceptions into account. Errors of this kind are called *overgeneralizations.* These systematic errors reveal the strategies the child is using to create language. The rules of the child's system can be inferred from the error patterns.

Some syntactical overgeneralizations may be familiar to you. English-speaking children quickly find the general rule for plurals: *Cat* becomes *cats, dog* becomes *dogs,* and so on. Having arrived at a way to construct plurals, a child will then say "I have two foots." *Foots* is an error resulting from a systematic attempt to apply the rule for plurals to all situations without taking exceptions into account.

On the phonological level, English-speaking children quickly learn that a word may have more than one syllable. They express that fact by repeating the first syllable or syllables (Ervin-Tripp, 1976). A small child is daunted by the word *refrigerator* and converts it to *freda-freda.* The child is saying "I can't quite manage it yet, but I know this word has more than one syllable."

In Spanish, the first-person form of a verb in the present tense results from dropping the infinitive ending and adding *-o* to the root. For example, *tomar* (to take) becomes *tomo* (I take); *comer* (to eat) becomes *como* (I eat). When you ask small children in Spanish if they know something, they often reply *sabo,* from the verb *saber* (to know). *Sabo* seems logically correct, but it is an error resulting from overgeneralization of a rule. The syntactically correct form is an exception to the rule. As children mature, they learn to say *sé.*

When children grasp the organizational principles underlying language, they can produce and understand novel utterances—things they have never heard or said before. Rules children generate sometimes produce language that differs from adult language. Child language, however, is neither haphazard nor an inept imitation of adult language. Child language is a system in itself—in fact, a series of systems, which gradually evolves into the adult form of the language.

## FIRST LANGUAGE DEVELOPMENT AND COMPREHENSIBLE INPUT

Chomsky originally proposed that LAD allowed children to make sense of the linguistic input they were receiving, even though that input was fragmented and confused.

Contrary to Chomsky's assertion that input is fragmented and confused, subsequent research indicates that linguistic input directed at children is in fact carefully organized (Macaulay, 1980). This reversal of thinking about linguistic input is important. It moves the focus for the study of language acquisition from the biological component to the social component, which features the child and the provider of linguistic input as active participants in language development.

### Child-Directed Speech

Recent research has analyzed the special register used with children, sometimes called *child-directed speech, caretaker speech,* or *motherese.* In certain settings, it seems that mothers engage in a special kind of "conversation" with their babies while nursing them (Snow, 1977). Such a conversation might seem one-sided, with the mother doing most of the talking, except that mothers are exceptionally forgiving about what they will accept as a response. Initially, burping, yawning, sneezing, and other incidental sounds are acceptable to a mother as responses. Long before the emergence of the child's speech, these interactions between mother and infant apparently teach turn taking, a basic skill in human communication.

Apparently, adults and even other children modify their speech to encourage children's language development. Comprehensible input for children is provided through a variety of strategies such as:

- speaking slowly
- using simple vocabulary—in short, simple sentences
- avoiding pausing before the end of a sentence
- exaggerating intonation and raising voice pitch
- repetition

An instruction for an adult, for example, might be: "The cereal is on the second shelf to the left of the coffee." On the other hand, for a child, the same instruction might take this form: "See the red coffee can? Up on the shelf over the blue dishes? Yes, that one. The cereal is next to it. Good, you got it."

## The Social and Cultural Contexts of Language Acquisition

Research on caretaker speech, or motherese, as characterized above, has generally focused on middle-class English speakers (Peters, 1985). This focus is shifting as we begin to recognize that language learning is inseparable from culture learning. In an analysis of language acquisition among the Kaluli of Papua New Guinea, Schieffelin (1985) remarked, "Every society has its own ideology about language, including when it begins and how children acquire it" (p. 531).

Kaluli people (Schieffelin, 1985) assume that infants are incapable of understanding and they rarely address them directly except to use their names. It is assumed that children begin to speak when they use the single-syllable words for *mother* and *breast*. From that time on, children are instructed directly by their caretakers in how to respond to a third party. For example, if two children are playing, a Kaluli mother may instruct one to respond to the other, "Give me that," followed by the instruction, "Say like that."

Givón (1985) reports that the Utes, who are Northern Plains Indians in the United States, discourage interaction between adults and children. In general, people are not encouraged to speak out in council until they have reached the age of 40 or 50. It is not surprising, therefore, that Ute children are expected to listen and not talk to adults. Children receive most of their linguistic input from other children.

In other words, language acquisition is a subset of the larger socialization process. It is a particularly important subset because nearly everything we do involves language. What a child mainly learns through language is how to become a competent member of a particular society. The Kaluli and the Ute cultures illustrate that concepts about the nature of children, the nature of language, and therefore the nature of linguistic interaction, vary from one culture to another depending on values and beliefs.

## Input Modification

It is interesting to note that as the child's language develops, the strategies and modifications of adult language providers change (Garnica, 1977). As children mature, adults diminish the number of special cues and hints they provide to facilitate communication. Adults are remarkably patient with tiny infants, accepting even the sounds of body functions as responses in conversation. We are more demanding of toddlers, but still tolerant of the limits of their language ability. The older a child gets, the more we expect his or her language to approximate the norms of adult language.

Awareness of the modification of input for new language learners helps us develop strategies for second language instruction and content instruction in the second language. Linguistic modifications made consciously as part of an instructional program can assist students to gain competence in a second language.

## Stages of First Language Development

*Crying.* Children all over the world move through the same stages of language development. At first, children cry to express dissatisfaction. Crying is not speech, but it does have elements of speech, such as intonation, pattern, and pitch. Recent experimentation suggests that infants use the fussy transitional period between quietude and crying to explore their speech organs and discover new sound possibilities (Campbell-Jones, 1985). Between the ages of two and four months, babies add cooing—an expression of pleasure or satisfaction—to their repertoire.

*Babbling.* At about the age of five months, babies begin to babble. Babbling children are exploring the potential range of speech production, practicing using their speech organs, and controlling them via the brain. The sounds made by a babbling child are not particularly related to the sound of the language that child hears. All normal children are born with the same organs for speech production, and all babbling babies sound much the same.

The quality of babbling changes, however, at about the age of six months, when children begin echolalic babbling. At that stage, a child seems to produce with greater frequency the sounds that are prevalent in the language that he or she is hearing. There are conflicting views about the function of echolalic babbling, but it seems to be a ruling-out process, where the child eliminates those sounds that are not meaningful in the native language and attempts to imitate those sounds that are (Sachs, 1985).

*Telegraphic Speech.* Around the age of one year, children can produce a one-word utterance, and, at some time in the second year, speech expands to two-word utterances. These early utterances generally refer initially to the appearance or disappearance of something: "All-gone milk" is a concept that has significance for very young children. Psycholinguists have attempted to identify the relationship between cognitive and linguistic development. In general, they have concluded that children have to grasp a concept, or at least a rudimentary version of it, before they can produce the language for it (Gleason, 1985).

Meanings expand during the two-word stage, and children develop telegraphic speech. Telegraphic speech is abbreviated or elliptical in nature, like the language used in telegrams. Children in this stage rely on gestures to elaborate what they mean. For example, "Daddy up" may mean "daddy, wake up," "daddy, pick me up," "daddy, stand up," or any number of things, depending on the situation. After the two-word stage, children move to a three-word utterance stage. As the child's utterances grow longer, reliance on gestures diminishes, and complex grammatical forms develop. Figure 4.1 illustrates the stages of language development.

## Order of Acquisition

The stages of language development are universal and progress from the simple to the complex. Remember, however, that what may be simple in one language can be relatively complex in another. For example, in English, we can indicate that the book belongs to Mommy by saying "Mommy's book." In Yiddish, a highly inflected language, the construction changes to "the book of the Mommy," and the word for *Mommy* is altered to indicate that it has become an indirect object in the phrase. English-speaking children will learn to express possessive forms earlier than their Yiddish-speaking peers.

A normal child enters kindergarten with a vocabulary of approximately 8,000 words and an excellent grasp of syntax, providing the foundation for the language and literacy development that will follow in school. This accomplishment provides a strong rationale for providing primary language instruction

**FIGURE 4.1.**  The stages of first language development. (Note that every child develops at a different rate. Ages are always approximate.)

| Age | Language Accomplishment | Examples | |
|---|---|---|---|
| 0–2 months | Crying (expresses discomfort) | | |
| 2–4 months | Cooing (expresses satisfaction or pleasure) | aaa, ooo | |
| 4–9 months | Babbling, changing to echolalic babbling | gagaga, mamamama | |
| 9–18 months | One-word utterances | milk | |
| 18 months– 2½ years | Two-word utterances; the beginning of syntax, expanding to three-word utterances | more milk baby up now | |
| 2½–4 years | Expanded syntax and vocabulary | I eated the cookie | |

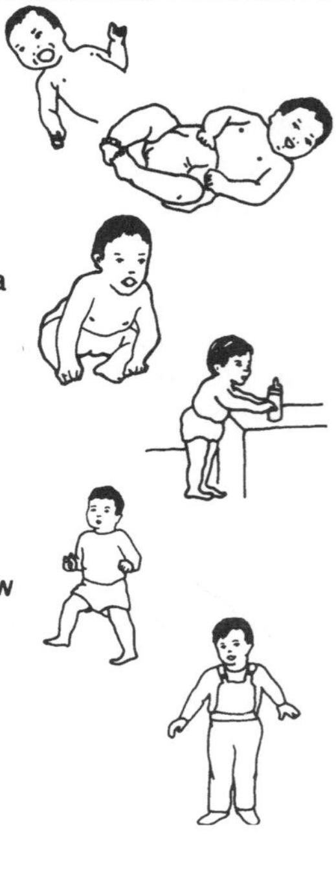

in the early grades. As we will see, it is logical to begin early skill instruction in that language, building on the conceptual and linguistic framework the child brings to school.

## Children as Sociolinguists

Like adults, children alter their language to respond to the setting, the function of the interaction, and the relative status of the individuals involved. For example, children differentiate between formal and informal speech, possibly as the result of the emphasis adults place on politeness.

Children also assign different language characteristics to males and females. While most evidence of gender-related speech differences is anecdotal rather than empirical, we do know that there are societal stereotypes regarding language and gender. As early as preschool, children participate in common stereotypical expectations about how males and females use language. For example, using puppets and role playing, researchers found that young children consider tag questions and indirect requests to be appropriate for females and associate direct and competitive speech with males (for a review, see Warren-Leubecker & Bohannon, 1985).

Bilingual children develop a keen sense of the relative prestige of their two languages (Saville-Troike, 1976). Teachers must be aware of the relative status of the languages they use in a dual language setting, so as to counteract the negative biases children may bring to the classroom (Legarreta-Marcaida, 1981). This is an important point, which we will investigate further in Chapter 5.

## SECOND LANGUAGE ACQUISITION

How do people learn a second language? Do they rely mainly on transferring knowledge from their first language to their second? Or do they recapitulate first language development, sorting out the organizing principles of their new language as they are exposed to it?

Proponents of the transfer approach have analyzed the errors people make in their second language to see if they are the result of interference from the old habits of their first. Proponents of the developmental position look for evidence that learners engage in a rule-finding process as they acquire their second language. Understanding the process of second language acquisition is useful to dual language teachers because it can provide insights into ways to structure effective second language instruction.

Researchers in the area of second language acquisition have discovered that the process is quite complex because language learning is a multifaceted problem-solving activity. Much as they would approach any problem, people approach language learning using the information and abilities they already have. Using first language knowledge and skills may produce errors that resemble interference but which are, in fact, evidence of a creative cognitive strategy for solving the new language puzzle. In other words, transfer of language information may be part of the process. In addition, evidence suggests that second language learners may also recapitulate the first language developmental process. The surface manifestations of that process, or the language they produce, may not resemble first language development at every stage, because the learners come to the process with useful prior knowledge and cognitive maturity.

Given the many variables that might affect the process of second language acquisition, it is not surprising that researchers have launched their investigations from a variety of viewpoints. The following sections briefly discuss the possible effects of age, personality, and social setting on learning a second language. Remember, however, that these factors are artificially distinguished for study purposes. Our best understanding of second language acquisition indicates that the process involves an integration of psychological, social, and linguistic factors.

## The Effect of Age

It is generally assumed that children learn second languages better than adults do. Lenneberg (1967) lent credence to that notion when he proposed that a second language is best learned in the "critical period" between the age of two years and the onset of puberty. He suggested that the ability to learn languages is debilitated by the completion of a process of lateralization in the brain, when each side of the brain develops its own specialized functions. While the critical period idea is intuitively appealing, it should be noted that empirical research has focused primarily on pronunciation.

Later analysis suggests that children who learn their second language before puberty do in fact acquire native-like pronunciation—unlike adults, who usually speak a second language with an accent. Larsen-Freeman and Long (1991) summarize the research on the effect of age on second language acquisition, commenting "younger is better in the most crucial area, ultimate attainment, with only quite young (child starters) being able to achieve accent-free, native like performance. . . ." (p. 155).

The comparison of adults and children and the focus on pronunciation, however, obscure the real issue for educators. What is of interest to us is whether younger or older children are better at developing the kind of second language proficiency they need for school. And the answer to that question is complex. Collier (1987) points out, "It depends. It depends on the learner's cognitive style, socioeconomic background, formal schooling in first language, and many other factors" (p. 1). Collier goes on to conclude, however, that it is safe to say that children between the ages of 8 and 12 acquire a second language faster than children between the ages of 4 and 7, which may be related to cognitive maturity and first language competence. Children past the age of 12 seem to slow down, and that may be because the demands made on them in school are out of keeping with the level of language that they bring to bear. (See Chapter 5 for a discussion of Cognitive Academic Language Proficiency, the kind of language children need for school.)

## The Effect of Personality

If you have been a second language learner, you may have found on occasion that your ability to use the language is enhanced after you've had a glass of wine in a relaxed, informal setting. It may surprise you to know that researchers have also noticed this phenomenon and have actually studied the effect of alcohol on second language performance. This is not as silly as it may appear at first glance, because it would be useful for us to understand the role of personality factors like inhibitions in second language learning.

If you are a person who can easily shed your inhibitions, you may be willing to take some of the risks involved in trying out a new language. Other personality characteristics may also affect your ability to learn a second language. For example, if you are a person with strong self-esteem, you may be well equipped to withstand some of the embarrassment that naturally occurs when you make language errors. If you are naturally outgoing, you may be likely to become involved in situations where you can use and practice your new language and facilitate its development (Brown, 1987).

Some caution is called for here: In the first place, it is difficult to define personality traits. Even with operational definitions, personality traits are difficult to measure. Nevertheless, it seems clear that individual psychological traits have an effect on the ability to learn a second language.

## The Social Factors

Communication is at the heart of language, and the need to establish communication is a powerful motivation for language development. Therefore, it is essential to consider the nature of interaction between people in social contexts and the effects of that interaction on second language acquisition.

In first language development, for example, it has been noted that motherese, or caretaker speech, is often ungrammatical. In one well-known study (Brown, Cazden, & Bellugi, 1973), it was found that parents do not correct statements made by their children if they are grammatically deficient but do correct them if they are untrue. In other words, parents are more concerned with the content of communication than with form.

Richard-Amato (1988) points out: "When the child says 'Daddy home' for the first time, no one labels this a mistake. . . . Instead it is thought of as being ingenious and cute and the child is hugged or rewarded verbally" (p. 36). Caretakers are delighted by a child's verbalizations and are anxious to promote interaction that may facilitate language development. Likewise, in situations with second language learners or speakers, native speakers may alter or modify their speech to facilitate understanding and response. This has been called *foreigner-talk*. In general, second language learners may do well in settings that emphasize communication.

One observer (Seliger, 1977) has noted that small children will participate in and appear to enjoy interactions that may be difficult or impossible for them to comprehend, which may function as a way of generating input. It is possible that the inclination to initiate and maintain interaction may be a strategy that distinguishes successful second language learners. In other words, some people may be better than others at creating situations that generate input, which brings us back to the question of the effect of personality on language ability and demonstrates the links between the social and psychological aspects of second language learning.

## INTEGRATIVE MODELS OF SECOND LANGUAGE ACQUISITION

Sufficient information on second language acquisition exists to enable us to formulate hypothetical models of the process. Models can then provide frameworks for additional research and coherent instructional programs. The sections that follow discuss two theoretical approaches to second language acquisition. These are but a small sample of the ways this process has been analyzed, but the two theories described here are useful because they integrate psychological and social considerations.

### The Acquisition-Learning Distinction

Stephen Krashen (1981) has proposed a distinction between *language acquisition* and *language learning.* Language acquisition, in informal terms, is picking up a language—learning it unconsciously from the social environment. Language learning, on the other hand, is learning a language or about a language in a formal sense—for example, in a classroom setting. According to Krashen's theory, children develop language through acquisition, by understanding language that is a little beyond their capabilities, presented by language providers who communicate with the child in a modified form.

These small increments of language, available to the learner when they are embedded in comprehensible input, are particularly accessible in nonthreatening, low-anxiety situations. Krashen refers to the affective component of language learning as an *affective filter,* a kind of emotional barrier to language learning that must be lowered if acquisition is to take place.

Krashen suggests that language learning is different from language acquisition in the following way: Learning provides a *monitor,* which allows the learner to correct language output. This monitor, however, is useful only when the learner knows the appropriate language rule, has time to use it, and is focused on form, as in writing. In this framework, acquired language is viewed as more important and more useful than learned language in the quick give-and-take or ordinary communication. According to Krashen, in real communication situations, second language learners most often use the language they have acquired rather than the language they have learned.

The distinction between learning and acquisition, the concept of the monitor, and the role of affective considerations may shed light on some of the issues currently debated in second language theory. The theoretical distinction between learning and acquisition and the monitor construct provide keys to the process in general. Krashen's theory suggests that transfer errors, or errors that reflect first language structures, appear when an individual is relying on the monitor. To the extent that an individual functions in an acquired-language mode, "errors" will replicate developmental errors.

The model also suggests answers to questions about specific variables. For example, it addresses the concern about the relationship between age and the ability to gain a second language. In the short run, older learners seem to gain competence in a second language more rapidly than young children. The model suggests that they may be better monitor users. On the other hand, children outperform adults in second language in the long run. Krashen's theory suggests that children are less likely to rely too heavily on the monitor and are less prone to the anxiety that often accompanies second language learning. Similarly, individual variation in second language ability can be explained in terms of both individual ability to use a monitor appropriately and quickly and individual willingness to take risks and rely on acquired language.

Krashen's theory has gained tremendous popularity among classroom teachers and has led to the development of innovative methodology that moves significantly away from grammar-translation and other traditional approaches. (The natural language approach, based on Krashen's theory, is discussed in Chapter 7.) At the same time, Krashen has drawn fire from critics of the model (Ellis, 1988; Larsen-Freeman & Long, 1991) who suggest that it is flawed by the following factors.

- The concept of an unbreachable distinction between acquisition and learning doesn't fit with what we already know about subconscious and conscious learning, which seem to exist on a continuum.
- Krashen doesn't really tell us what goes on cognitively during acquisition and learning.
- We cannot empirically test either the acquisition-learning distinction or the monitor construct.

Finally, Krashen's model is misleading because it places more emphasis on the importance of input than output. Output is a necessary condition of interaction; but in Krashen's view, hypothesis testing is an internal process whereby learners match up input with the knowledge they already have about the language. In other words, the theory doesn't give enough credit to the dynamic interaction between the language learner and the social environment. The next section describes a theory that recognizes the role of input in second language acquisition but places interaction in a central role.

## Language Learners and Language Speakers Interact

Lily Wong Fillmore (1985) suggests that three components are necessary for an effective language learning situation:

- the learners
- the speakers of the language the learner wants to learn
- the social setting that brings learners and speakers together

Once the learners and the speakers have been brought together, three types of interactive processes take place. First, there are social processes. In social processes, learners assume that the language used is relevant to the immediate situation, and speakers cooperate with that assumption. Second, there are linguistic processes. Learners use what they already know about language to try to make sense out of the linguistic input they receive. And third, there are cognitive strategies that learners use to figure out the relationships between what is happening and the language being used.

Finally, Wong Fillmore (1991) suggests that the ability of language learners to utilize strategies is affected by the social context. She also emphasizes that all the factors are interrelated, and proposes situations where the contact with speakers of the target language and consequently the amount and type of input a learner receives may be related to the age of the learner.

For example, in the United States, young newcomers attend school, where they are likely to meet English speakers and to have classroom experiences that provide them with comprehensible input in English. Older immigrants, however, often find jobs where co-workers share their primary language, which limits their exposure to English. Also, older learners may find it harder than younger ones to get the kind of interaction they need to develop a new language. Young children can manage their social interactions with language that is not very complex. In fact, very young children often play happily together even though they may not understand each other's language. Adults, on the other hand, cannot participate fully in social interaction without the use of language, so beginning speakers are at a social disadvantage.

Wong Fillmore's model proposes that variations in language learning may result from a complex relationship of differences in individual personalities, cognitive abilities, and social skills, as well as from the social context itself. Wong Fillmore's analysis emphasizes the dynamic role of social interaction in second language learning.

## SUMMARY

Traditionally, it was assumed that children developed language through imitation and habit formation. Chomsky revolutionized thinking about language development by theorizing that we can explain original utterances only by assuming that children have an innate language learning device that enables them to deduce the rules of syntax. Subsequent theorists have suggested that children apply this rule-finding approach to the semantic and pragmatic systems of language as well.

Theorists in second language acquisition ask whether second languages are acquired by transfer of first language knowledge or through a developmental process that parallels first language acquisition. Krashen distinguishes between language learning and language acquisition in an attempt to explain why some research produces evidence of transfer and other research substantiates the developmental process in second language development. Wong Fillmore suggests that learners make use of cognitive, linguistic, and social strategies during social interactions to acquire a new language.

First language development and second language acquisition theories will enable teachers in dual language settings to make decisions about methodologies for first language development and second language instruction.

## ACTIVITIES AND QUESTIONS TO THINK ABOUT

1. Tape record an interaction between a child between the ages of one and three, and the child's parent. Identify the strategies the parent uses to facilitate the communication. For example, how does the parent acknowledge the child's role in the conversation? Does the parent repeat what the child says? paraphrase or elaborate on the child's contribution? Identify any strategies the child uses to maintain or prolong the interaction. What stage of language development has the child reached? Give examples that support your choice.

2. Visit a classroom and observe an English as a second language lesson. Note the materials and the methods. What assumptions are being made in this setting about how people learn language? For example, does instruction mainly consist of oral pattern drills? completion of grammar exercises?

3. Interview an immigrant who is learning English as a second language. How does this person view the process of second language learning: Is this person taking classes or learning the language informally? Is the process easy or difficult? What is the most difficult part of the process? In this person's view, what factors have facilitated the process; that is, what helped the most?

## SUGGESTIONS FOR FURTHER READING

Bialystok, E. (Ed.) (1991). *Language processing in bilingual children.* Cambridge, Eng.: Cambridge University Press.
   The articles in this book contain descriptions of original research on bilingual children's acquisition of language. The chapter by Wong Fillmore is an excellent summary of her longitudinal research and the conclusions she has drawn from it.

Brown, H. D. (1987). *Principles of language learning and teaching* (2nd ed.). Englewood Cliffs, NJ: Prentice-Hall.

An update of a well-known book on second language learning, this edition provides clear, concise explanations of theories of second language acquisition. The book is enhanced by the addition of an "in the classroom" section at the end of each chapter which highlights second language teaching methodologies.

de Villiers, P. A., & de Villiers, J. G. (1979). *Early language.* Cambridge, MA: Harvard University Press.

An easy to read, straightforward discussion of the course of language development, this book is enlivened by samples of children's language.

Gleason, J. B. (Ed.). (1985). *The development of language.* Columbus, OH: Merrill.

Ten articles which provide an overview of theory and research of first language development across the entire life span. The chapter on language in society (Warren-Leubecker & Bohannon) is an excellent summary of research regarding acquisition of the social rules of language.

Larsen-Freeman, D., & Long, M. H. (1991). *An introduction to second language research.* White Plains, NY: Longman.

Just about everything you wanted to know about second language acquisition is included in this well-organized book, which explains second language acquisition research methods, describes and critiques prevailing theories, and discusses implications for instruction.

Lightbown, P., & Spada, N. (1993). *How languages are learned.* Oxford: Oxford University Press.

Contains an overview of theories of first language development and second language acquisition, followed by a discussion of approaches to teaching second language which emphasizes the relevance of research to practice.

Ventriglia, L. (1982). *Conversations of Miguel and Maria: How children learn English as a second language: Implications for classroom teaching.* Reading, MA: Addison-Wesley.

Based on analysis of children's conversations, this book analyzes second language acquisition strategies and presents classroom methods based on those strategies. Emphasis is on the importance of social context in second language acquisition.

# chapter 5

# Language Ability

$G$iven the complexity of language and its development, it should not be surprising that the assessment of language skills presents complex and often unresolved issues. In this chapter we will look at communicative competence and strategies for assessing language ability. We will also consider the meaning of bilingualism and its impact on intellectual and academic development.

## WHAT IS COMMUNICATIVE COMPETENCE?

Over the years, many of my students have expressed discomfort about their accents in a second language. However, after listening to and discussing several taped samples of people who speak English as a second language, they generally agree that accent and even syntax are not the keys to a person's ability to speak a language. Even this brief and rather superficial exercise leads us to thinking about communicative competence. What are the factors that enable a person actually to use a language in a way that fulfills its main purpose—communication?

### Models of Language Proficiency

Some theorists employ complex concepts to define and describe the ability to use language. One model cross-references linguistic and sociolinguistic components with comprehension, production, reading, and writing to produce a grid with 64 measurable intersections of proficiency (Hernandez-Chavez, Burt, & Dulay, 1978).

A more succinct framework identifies four components of communicative competence (Canale & Swain, 1980):

- grammatical competence, or mastery of the sound system of a language, its syntax, and its semantics, plus knowledge of vocabulary
- sociolinguistic competence, which includes mastery of the use of appropriate forms, registers, and styles of language for different social contexts
- discourse competence, which involves the ability to connect utterances in a meaningful way and relate them appropriately to a topic
- strategic competence, or the ability to compensate for breakdowns in communication

## Communication and Language in School

Because such theories fail to account for the developmental relationship between a student's first and second languages, these and similar models of communicative competence have been criticized as inapplicable to minority students' acquisition of English. Native speakers acquire language skills in a predictable order, but the same order of acquisition may not apply to the acquisition of a second language. As we saw in Chapter 4, second language acquisition may depend on a number of variables, including age and previous schooling. For example, a person may master literacy skills in a second language without ever completely mastering its pronunciation, or vice versa.

Apart from developmental considerations, these general theories of communicative competence fail to take into account the particularities of the school setting, where both the required tasks and the style of communication differ significantly from other daily experiences and communication. Jim Cummins (1994) has formulated a model of language proficiency that accounts for the demands of the classroom.

*Cognitively Demanding Tasks.*    In school, many tasks required of children are new. New tasks tend to be cognitively demanding; that is, they require more thinking. As a task becomes more familiar, it becomes cognitively less demanding and requires less thinking. Reflect for a moment on your own experience of learning to drive. At the outset, driving was probably a demanding task that required a great deal of your attention. If you have been driving for some time, however, you probably do so quite automatically. Practice has made this a cognitively undemanding task. Similarly, reading is generally an automatic skill for most adults. Children who are learning to read, however, are engaged in a cognitively demanding activity.

***Communication and Context.*** Communication can be described on a continuum from context-embedded to context-reduced (Cummins, 1994). Context-embedded communication takes place in the presence of environmental clues. For example, you may have traveled and shopped in a place where you knew little or none of the local language. You were probably able to make your purchases by communicating with gestures and intonation, especially since you and the shopkeeper shared certain assumptions about the nature and purpose of your interaction. In other words, your transaction was supported by context clues.

Context-reduced communication, on the other hand, takes place in the absence of context clues. Most classroom communication is context-reduced. Much as we may try to mediate our lessons with hands-on activities, objects, and illustrations, we are often several steps removed from real-life experience. It is possible, of course, for a class to discuss the weather using context clues such as the students' clothing or an illustrative chart, because weather is concrete and visible. It is far more difficult, however, to provide context clues for abstract concepts such as democracy or photosynthesis.

***Language Proficiency in School Settings.*** The outcome of cross-referencing the intensity of context with the level of cognitive demand can be illustrated with the simple diagram shown in Figure 5.1.

Much of what takes place in classrooms falls in quadrant D of the diagram. In other words, what happens in classrooms is often context-reduced and relies heavily on written and verbal explanations in the absence of concrete clues. In addition, classroom tasks are generally cognitively demanding, requiring students to focus on tasks that are new and challenging. According to Cummins, in

**FIGURE 5.1.** Context and cognitive load

SOURCE: J. Cummins, "The Role of Primary Language Development in Promoting Educational Success for Language Minority Students." In California State Department of Education (Ed.), *Schooling and Language Minority Students: A Theoretical Framework* (Los Angeles: Evaluation, Dissemination and Assessment Center, California State University, Los Angeles, 2nd ed., 1994, p. 12.)

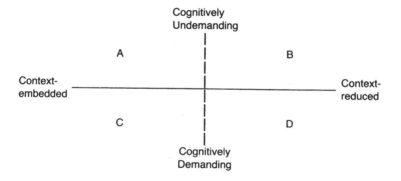

order to properly assess students' language ability, it is useful to distinguish between two types of language proficiency:

- *Basic Interpersonal Communicative Skills (BICS):* the language skills required for face-to-face communication, where interactions are context-embedded
- *Cognitive/Academic Language Proficiency (CALP):* the language skills required for academic achievement in a context-reduced environment

Limited English proficient children quickly acquire BICS in English from their playmates, the media, and their day-to-day experiences, but in assessing their language proficiency we must recognize the distinction between those skills and CALP. The language skills required in any classroom are context-specific and quite different from the basic skills necessary for everyday communication. If we fail to recognize this difference, we may erroneously assume that children have acquired sufficient proficiency in English to succeed in a classroom where only English is used, when in fact they have not.

The distinction between BICS and CALP is not the only theoretical approach to describing language proficiency. The terminology, however, has become popular among practitioners. Cummins's theory has nurtured an awareness that the dynamics of school-related language proficiency is important for an understanding of the rationale for providing academic support in a student's first language as part of the instructional program (see Chapter 6).

## HOW IS LANGUAGE PROFICIENCY ASSESSED?

Language assessment is a critical aspect of dual language instruction. Knowledge about a student's language abilities is essential for placement in an appropriate program. Generally, language proficiency is assessed using standardized tests. Language proficiency tests may be categorized according to the nature of the tasks they involve and the way they are scored.

- *Discrete point tests:* Based on the assumption that language is the sum of discrete structural units such as phonemes and morphemes, these tests assess mastery of each of the units (Day, McCollum, Cieslak, & Erickson, 1981). For example, a discrete point test might assess phonological ability by asking a student to distinguish between minimal pairs such as *ten* and *den.*
- *Integrative tests:* These tests attempt to assess an individual's ability to use a language for communication. This requires an assessment of a student's understanding of both the linguistic and social contexts of a language.

It is possible for a test to require tasks that involve natural and spontaneous language production, which is then scored in a discrete point fashion. For a test to be truly integrative, it should be scored globally, with emphasis on the ability to communicate.

## Discrete Point Tests

Discrete point tests are the least favored in current thinking about communicative competence. Discrete point testing has its roots in the structural linguistic approaches of the 1950s, which emphasized language acquisition as the development of habits across language structures such as phonemes, morphemes, and syntax. Discrete point tests are not generally measures of communicative competence. Second language instructors are often frustrated when students who score well on a language assessment test are not capable of using the language in real-life situations (Day, McCollum, Cieslak, & Erickson, 1981).

*Why Are Discrete Point Tests Used?* Despite the inadequacies of discrete point tests, they are often used in schools. Reasons for this may be:

- *Theoretical:* Selection of assessment instruments in some districts may have been made at a time when research in the areas of language acquisition and bilingualism was relatively new.
- *Political:* Legislative mandates for assessment of large numbers of non-English-speaking children required hasty responses on the part of school districts.
- *Practical:* The need to serve large numbers of children may have led districts to select assessment instruments that were simple to administer. Also, large-scale testing is expensive. Once a district has made a commitment to a test, a change may be economically unfeasible.

## Integrative Tests: Assessing Communication

Most of the tasks that discrete point tests generally comprise never come up in ordinary discourse. It is unlikely, for example, that anyone would ever ask you to convert a list of nouns into their plural forms in the course of an everyday conversation. But what kinds of tasks can actually demonstrate an individual's understanding of a language and its social context?

Surprisingly, research indicates that dictation is a useful measure of a person's overall language ability. Apparently, the ability to divide up and write down what you hear when you take dictation requires an understanding of meaning. Dictation selections used to assess language ability must approximate normal discourse and should be presented in sequences that are long enough to challenge a student's short-term memory.

Another integrative technique for assessing language ability is cloze testing. A cloze task requires the test taker to fill in the blanks in a passage where words have been left out. It is possible to adapt cloze techniques for children by presenting passages orally.

There are a variety of oral production tasks that can be effective for eliciting language samples from young students to provide material for an assessment. Apart from structured interviews, students can be asked to retell a story, or to describe a craft project they have completed using materials supplied by the examiner. In whatever manner an oral production task is structured, it should, as much as possible, motivate spontaneous conversation.

Despite its usefulness, integrative testing is not as common as discrete point testing. Integrative testing is often time-consuming and may require extensive training for test administrators. Also, the concept of global scoring is perceived by many educators as subjective and therefore risky.

## Other Issues in Language Assessment

There are several other concerns about language proficiency assessment in general.

*Culture Bias.*    Cultural bias in both content and procedure may exist in language proficiency tests. Content bias includes items where the "correct" answer reflects the values and experiences of a particular normative group, generally the white middle class. Cheng (1987) notes, for example, that children from various Asian language backgrounds may be unfamiliar with utensils commonly used in the United States for baking, fitted sheets, pumpkin pie, and a whole host of objects, events, people and ideas that are part of American culture. Test procedures may also be culturally biased. Expectations, for example, that children will speak up when addressed or offer elaborated information in response to a question are not appropriate in every culture.

*The Testing Situation.*    Language proficiency testing situations may be threatening for particular children or cultural groups. Even a very verbal child may refuse to speak freely to a stranger or a person in authority. A thorough assessment of a child's abilities should include observations made by a teacher over time, in a variety of settings.

*The Need for a Multidimensional Approach to Assessment.*    Formal language proficiency assessment for elementary school children is often limited to assessment of their proficiency in English. Such assessments are incomplete and fail to identify potential strengths and weaknesses. A child who is proficient in English may be proficient in another language as well. A child who is deficient in English may be proficient in another language. A child who is deficient in more than one language may have special needs.

In addition, any given language test is but one sample of an individual's language performance. We know that performance differs from competence and that we can only infer competence from performance. Furthermore, as we have seen, there are many factors that might affect any particular performance. Therefore, language proficiency assessments should include multiple measures. Both discrete point and integrative tests can be useful. In addition, informal teacher observations over time may be far more accurate than any particular test. Multidimensional assessments are needed in order to profile a child's full linguistic repertoire.

## WHAT IS BILINGUALISM?

Information about the number of languages in the world and the numbers of speakers of those languages is readily available. There is little information, however, regarding the number of people in the world who are bilingual or multilingual. It would be difficult for a researcher to collect that information, since theorists have defined *bilingualism* in many different ways.

A strict definition of *bilingualism* suggests that a bilingual person has native-like control of two languages (Bloomfield, 1933). Yet while many of the readers of this book undoubtedly function in more than one language, probably few would claim native-like capability in each language in every situation. Discussions with multilingual people reveal that they make choices about language use that are affected by the setting and function of the particular interaction (Miller, 1983). People who function in two or more languages know that those who have equal and highly developed capacity in two or more languages are relatively rare and generally much admired.

Grosjean, in *Life with Two Languages* (1982), surveyed monolingual and bilingual college students to find out how they interpreted the term *bilingual*. He asked them: "If someone told you that X was bilingual in English and French, what would you understand by that?" (p. 231). In this survey, both monolingual and bilingual students indicated that *bilingual* means speaking two languages, and high ratings were given by both groups for the description "fluent in two languages." Unlike monolingual students in the study, however, bilingual students gave a high rating to "regular use of two languages." In that regard, bilingual students agree with many modern theorists who tend to favor the idea that use of two languages, rather than fluency, is the hallmark of bilingualism.

## CODE-SWITCHING

Bilinguals sometimes alternate the use of two languages from sentence to sentence, or even within one sentence. *Code-switching,* as this is called, may be misinterpreted by monolinguals as an inability on the part of a bilingual individual to speak either language properly.

Analysis by linguists and sociolinguists, however, has demonstrated that code-switching is a systematic and rule-governed language behavior. Within certain linguistic constraints, bilinguals may code-switch to:

- fill a lexical need: "*Le puse al niño en el* daycare."
- emphasize a point: "Get up now. *¡Levántate!*"
- express ethnic solidarity: "*Andale pues;* let's get together soon."

Other reasons for code-switching may include the desire to convey emotional or personal involvement, to include or exclude someone from a conversation, and to assert the status of the speaker (Grosjean, 1982).

In general, a person who code-switches demonstrates linguistic creativity and sophistication. However, a second type of code-switching, called *regressive code-switching* (Gonzalez & Maez, 1980), occurs in children who are losing their first language and leaning on their second language to supply missing elements. This kind of situation raises a pedagogical issue: Should teachers code-switch in dual language classrooms or keep the languages entirely separate?

Experts generally agree that teachers should restrict code-switching to the intersentential type. That is, teachers should switch languages only from sentence to sentence and not intrasententially, or within a sentence. They should, however, accept intrasentential code-switching by their students (Ovando & Collier, 1985). There is some evidence, however, that complete separation of the two languages of instruction is beneficial to the development of both (Cummins & Swain, 1986). Concurrent use of language in the classroom and other instructional models are discussed in Chapter 4.

## BILINGUALISM: A HANDICAP OR A TALENT?

Research prior to the 1960s tended to support the notion that bilingual children did poorly in school, and bilingualism was generally regarded as an academic handicap. Later analysis of those early findings reveals that the studies were biased against ethnic minority students. Investigators failed to take into account other variables such as social and economic factors; also, tests were usually administered only in English.

The assumption that bilingualism was a handicap led to unfortunate practices such as punishing children for using languages other than English in school, even at play. Rejection of a child's language—and, by implication, culture—adversely affects that child's self-concept and chances for academic success. In retrospect, the bilingualism-as-handicap position can be seen as a self-fulfilling prophecy.

Despite suggestions that early research on bilingualism may have been methodologically flawed, there have been recent studies that support the conclusions of earlier work and show that bilingual children score lower on verbal tests of intelligence or academic achievement than their monolingual counterparts. Other studies, however, indicate that bilingual children perform better than monolinguals on tests of linguistic skills, divergent thinking, sensitivity to communication, and general intelligence. (See Cummins & Swain, 1986, for a review.) How can we explain this apparent contradiction?

Quite simply, children can be enriched by knowing more than one language as long as they are *additive* rather than *subtractive* bilinguals. An additive bilingual has learned a second language in addition to the first, whereas a subtractive bilingual has gradually lost one language while acquiring a second. The distinction is significant from a pedagogical viewpoint because research indicates that children with high levels of proficiency in two languages show "positive cognitive effects" (Cummins, 1981, p. 39). In effect, children who come to school speaking more than one language or who learn a second language in school will benefit academically as long as both languages are nurtured and developed to the fullest extent.

## SUMMARY

The ability to use a language goes beyond the ability to manage its structural components. Communicative competence includes the ability to use a language in appropriate ways in various social contexts. Communicative competence in school includes Cognitive Academic Language Proficiency (CALP), the ability to function in context-reduced settings, where situational clues are minimal.

Communicative competence is difficult to assess. Many tests used to assess language ability focus on structural aspects of language to the exclusion of its social aspects.

There have been various definitions of bilingualism, with general agreement that it is related to the use of two languages. Bilinguals may code-switch, alternating the use of two languages in the same sentence or between sentences. This is generally systematic and indicates linguistic sophistication. Code-switching among children who are learning a second language, however, may indicate first language loss.

Some research indicates that bilingualism is an educational handicap. Recent studies, however, provide evidence that bilingualism enhances academic success when it is additive rather than subtractive in nature.

## ACTIVITIES AND QUESTIONS TO THINK ABOUT

1. Tape record a speaker of English as a second language in an informal conversation. Analyze the language sample from a structural perspective: Does the speaker have a noticeable foreign accent? Is the speaker's syntax close to native standards? Apart from your observations about structure, how would you rate this speaker's overall communicative competence? Share your samples with your classmates. Discuss your conclusions.

2. Obtain a copy of a language assessment instrument used in an educational setting in your area. Consider the following:

   - What are the steps for administering the test? Who may administer it? Is special training required to administer it? How long does it take to administer?
   - What is the theoretical rationale for the test? Are the tasks discrete point or integrative? Is the scoring discrete point or global?
   - Is this test used alone or in combination with other measures?
   - Do you consider this test appropriate for assessing the language ability of children in a dual language program? Why or why not?
   - What kinds of decisions are made based on the results of this test?

3. Talk to people who speak more than one language about their experience and understanding of bilingualism. What do they think *bilingual* means? How did they learn their languages? Which languages do they use for different situations? What attitudes do they have about their languages? about bilingualism in general?

## SUGGESTIONS FOR FURTHER READING

Cheng, L. L. (1987). *Assessing Asian language performance: Guidelines for evaluating limited-English-proficient students.* Rockville, MD: Aspen Publishers.
In addition to an overview of issues related to language proficiency testing in general, this book focuses on Asian language background children and discusses the needs of speakers of Chinese, Vietnamese, Laotian, Hmong, Cambodian, Filipino, Korean, Japanese, Hawaiian, and Chamorro.

Cohen, A. D. (1980). *Testing language ability in the classroom.* Rowley, MA: Newbury House.
This book attempts to meet the needs of the second language teacher on a daily basis. It contains practical information about test construction and discusses approaches to testing functional language ability.

Erickson, J. G., & Omark, D. R. (1981). *Communication assessment of the bilingual bicultural child: Issues and guidelines.* Baltimore: University Park Press.
A discussion of issues and procedures in language assessment, this book analyzes differences between discrete point, quasi-integrative, and integrative tests. Appendix C contains an annotated bibliography on the communication assessment of the bilingual child.

Miller, J. (1983). *Many voices: Bilingualism culture and education.* London: Routledge & Kegan Paul.
A fascinating recounting of the bilingual experience, explicated through interviews with a variety of multilingual subjects, who express their perceptions about their languages, how they learned them, and the ways they use them.

Oller, J. W., Jr. (1979). *Language tests at school.* White Plains, NY: Longman.
A theoretical framework for the development of what the author calls *pragmatic tests,* or tests of communicative competence, this book overviews theories and methods of language testing and provides guidelines for test development. Readers will find this a most useful introduction to testing concepts in general. Discussion questions at the end of each chapter are lively and provocative.

Savignon, S. J. (1983). *Communicative competence: Theory and classroom practice.* Reading, MA: Addison-Wesley.
Designed as a methods book for second language teaching, this book provides excellent theoretical background on language acquisition, communicative competence, and language assessment.

# chapter 6

# Primary Language Instruction for Limited English Proficient Students

**A**manda is a second-grade student in a private school in an affluent suburban area. Her father is a computer software engineer, and her mother is an attorney. In school, Amanda receives instruction in her subject areas in English; she studies French as a second language. In second grade, French is also used for art and social studies as well as related cultural activities and events. As Amanda progresses toward sixth grade, her French instruction will increase and she will develop speaking, reading, and writing skills.

Lilia was born in the United States of parents who were born in Mexico and speak no English. Lilia attends second grade in a public school in an economically disadvantaged urban area. When she entered kindergarten, Lilia was assessed as limited English proficient. She is enrolled in a program that offers her subject area instruction in Spanish, accompanied by daily classes in English as a second language. In addition, Lilia receives social studies and physical education instruction in English and participates in schoolwide activities and assemblies where English is used. As soon as Lilia can score above the 37th percentile on a standardized achievement test administered in English, she will be placed in a classroom where no Spanish is used.

Few people question the value of additive bilingualism for English-speaking children. Amanda's friends and family are impressed by her ability to speak French, and many have expressed the wish that they had received a comparable education. But controversy surrounds the idea of providing public school instruction for limited English proficient students in their native language while they learn English as a second language. Lilia is expected, appropriately, to learn English. While she may maintain her ability to speak Spanish, it is unlikely that she will ever become fully bilingual and biliterate. This subtractive bilingual scenario will not only limit her abilities in Spanish, but may have a negative impact on her abilities in English as well.

This chapter will present a five-point rationale for providing primary language instruction for limited English proficient children and will outline instructional approaches for implementing primary language support in the classroom.

## A RATIONALE FOR PRIMARY LANGUAGE INSTRUCTION

### Transfer of Concepts and Skills

The construction of a rationale for primary language instruction can be approached from several directions. We will begin by responding to the often-expressed criticism that classroom time spent in the primary language is wasteful. That idea is based on the assumption that languages are learned and maintained separately in the human brain. There is no evidence to support that model of language learning, which has been called the *Separate Underlying Proficiency model* (Cummins, 1994). In fact, research supports the opposite notion, or *Common Underlying Proficiency model* of language learning, which assumes that skills and concepts learned in one language transfer to another.

***How Does Transfer Work?***   Reading is an illustration of an area where there is significant transfer of behaviors, skills, knowledge, and attitudes from one language to another. A detailed analysis of the skills and subskills which constitute literacy would be out of place here, but consider a few of the concepts that provide the foundation for reading. You may find it difficult at first to identify them, because reading is highly automatic for literate adults!

Look at Figure 6.1, and try to read the Hebrew word. You are given some hints about direction and about sound-symbol correspondence. As you worked out the word, were you engaged in learning to read? Perhaps this exercise— using a language with an unfamiliar alphabet—has demonstrated that when you read in a new language, you apply literacy skills you already have to language-specific information.

Now consider some of the components of reading. Reading requires the understanding that print carries meaning. We develop this awareness in children through reading-readiness instruction. We read to them, point out signs and other sources of information in print, label objects in the classroom, and teach them to read and write their names.

Other prereading skills include directionality, sequencing, and the ability to distinguish among shapes and sounds. Those skills are not language bound; they transfer, as does the knowledge that written symbols correspond to sounds and can be decoded in a particular direction and order.

Hebrew may seem baffling to many of you because it uses an unfamiliar alphabet. Using the language-specific information provided, try to read the Hebrew word. After you have read it, think about the literacy skills you already have that helped you.

Language-specific Information:

- *Direction*—Read Hebrew from right to left.
- *Sequence*—Some vowels are placed under consonants.

Read the consonant first, and then the vowel.

- *Sounds and symbols*—Here are some correspondences that you will need to know:

שׁ = sh, as in shoe

ל = l, as in lamp

ם = m, as in mouse

ָ = o, as in tonic or cot

ֹ = o, as in home or bone

Try to read this word (turn the page upside down for the answer):

שָׁלוֹם

The word you read is "shalom," which means "greetings," or "peace."

**FIGURE 6.1.** Reading a new language

In addition to basic skills, reading habits and attitudes have a significant impact on an individual's ability to read. A sense of being a literate, capable person who can listen, concentrate, and complete a task transfers from one language to another (Thonis, 1983).

Reading is only one of the many areas where transfer from one language to another is significant. Content areas can be studied in any language, and the concepts are added to the common underlying cognitive store. From a pedagogical viewpoint, the message is clear. Instructional time spent in a child's primary language is not wasted. Skills, concepts, and knowledge acquired in one's first language will be readily available in one's second.

## Primary Language Development and Second Language Acquisition

Providing instruction in a child's primary language enhances acquisition of a second language. Unlike the notion of transfer, this idea seems counter-intuitive, and yet it is a related concept, grounded in the Common Underlying Proficiency model.

Research has demonstrated (see Cummins, 1981, for a review) that older immigrant children, with substantial educational preparation in their own language, fare better in achieving second language proficiency than younger immigrant children. Evidently, the older children have a well-developed conceptual base in their primary language as a result of their previous schooling and literacy. Learning a second language, for them, is a matter of translating concepts and ideas that are already firmly established. They need only learn new labels, unlike younger children, who face the more difficult task of having to learn basic concepts in a new and unfamiliar language.

For example, basic concepts involving spatial relationships often are reinforced in preschool or kindergarten as part of prereading and early mathematics. For small children, concepts like *over, under, behind,* and *around* may be unfamiliar. Learning them in a new language is difficult. For adults, who have internalized spatial relationships, they are relatively simple. Learning them in a new language requires only learning new words for relationships that have long become conceptually automatic.

The apparent contradiction that instructional time spent in a first language facilitates acquisition of a second is resolved by the Common Underlying Proficiency model. If we think in terms of a bank or reserve of language, with all deposits adding to the balance, we see quickly that a child who is poor in one language will be poor in another. Primary language instruction is the easiest way to increase a child's language wealth.

## Students Need to Develop CALP

In Chapter 5 we discussed the distinction between Basic Interpersonal Communicative Skills (BICS) and Cognitive Academic Language Proficiency (CALP), theoretical constructs developed by Cummins. BICS refers to the basic language skills necessary for communication in context-embedded settings, whereas CALP is the type of language proficiency needed to function in a classroom environment, where required tasks are context-reduced.

Students need to develop CALP in order to function adequately in academic situations. Relying on the ideas that concepts and skills transfer from one language to another and that students with a strong cognitive base will easily make the transition to a second language, the thesis that CALP should be developed in a student's first language follows.

Critics often suggest that language minority students should spend no more than three years in primary language programs. It takes, however, an average of five to seven years for children to develop CALP in any language (Cummins, 1981). Therefore, primary language instruction should be seen as more than a temporary vehicle for content coverage. For language minority children, primary language instruction is a tool for conceptual development that will enrich their ability to function in both first and second languages.

## Effects of Bilingualism on Achievement

It was suggested previously that early research in the field of bilingualism led to the conclusion that knowing more than one language is an educational handicap. Some recent studies, however, have indicated that bilingual children have greater cognitive flexibility and better language skills than monolingual children. This is logical, since bilingual children have more opportunities to play and work with language than do their monolingual counterparts.

Inconsistencies in studies on bilingualism have perplexed researchers for some time. The "threshold hypothesis" (Cummins, 1994) suggests that positive effects of bilingualism are associated with high levels of proficiency in more than one language. In other words, children who have acquired a high degree of proficiency in a second language while maintaining their abilities in a first show positive effects compared to those with partial or limited bilingualism. Once again, we are led to the conclusions that additive bilingualism has positive effects and that language minority children should be provided with instruction in their primary languages.

## Primary Language Instruction and Self-Concept

The notion of self-concept is intangible and complex. A person's self-concept is made up of an intricate network of factors, including the following:

- *Comparisons:* "How do I compare with other people?"
- *Perceptions of others:* "How do I think other people see me?"
- *Ideals:* "How would I be if I could be any way I choose?"

People develop their self-concept through the experiences they have with others. Some individuals have a particularly powerful impact on the self-concept of children. Parents play an important role in self-concept development, as do teachers (Amoriggi & Gefteas, 1981).

Children are natural sociologists and sociolinguists, well aware of attitudes in their environment regarding their culture and language. Children who perceive negative attitudes in the school setting toward their first language will become involved in subtractive bilingualism. Bilingualism is correlated to positive academic effects in situations where both languages have perceived value in the home and community (Cummins & Swain, 1986). Schools must promote the idea that the language children bring to school is prestigious and appropriate for use by educated people.

## OVERALL, WHAT DOES THE RESEARCH INDICATE?

There have been several attempts to evaluate the effects of bilingual programs on a large scale. Two well-known and often cited studies are a national evaluation of Title VII funded projects completed by the American Institute for Research (Danoff, Coles, McLaughlin, & Reynolds, 1977a, 1977b, 1978) and a study commissioned by the Office of Planning, Budget and Evaluation of the United States Department of Education (Baker & de Kanter, 1981).

Neither of those studies produced evidence favoring bilingual education, but both engendered heated controversy. Criticism has generally centered around research design and methodology. Two important factors call the results of the studies into question:

1. Many programs are labeled *bilingual,* but there may be a low degree of comparability among them. Immersion programs, as well as English as a second language pull-out programs, may be labeled *bilingual* by administrators seeking compliance with state and federal regulations or researchers who fail to understand the distinctions. In some areas, shortages of adequately trained staff result in assignment of monolingual teachers to "bilingual" classrooms where primary language support may be limited or nonexistent.

2. An effective research design requires that programs be randomly assigned to sites and then evaluated. There are no studies where this condition, called *random assignment to condition,* has been met. Consequently, program evaluation results are difficult to interpret.

The Baker and de Kanter analysis, which was actually a synthesis of 28 smaller studies, has been reanalyzed and compared using statistical processes that control for differences in the nature of the data (Willig, 1985). The reinterpretation provides evidence that supports bilingual education and the use of the primary language in the classroom.

Even so, for reasons we described, program research on the benefits of primary language instruction for language minority students is inconclusive. The issues are further clouded by politics. The U.S. Department of Education has repeatedly questioned the value of dual language instruction and has taken steps to expand funding for English-only programs. On the other hand, a report published by the U.S. General Accounting Office (1987a) supports dual language instruction.

Basic research on bilingualism, however, leaves little room for doubt as to the value of primary language instruction for language minority students (Hakuta, 1985). In communities that show a high regard for two languages and in educational programs that encourage additive bilingualism, knowing two languages is positively associated with intellectual and academic achievement (Cummins & Swain, 1986).

## IF PRIMARY LANGUAGE INSTRUCTION, THEN HOW?

Some experts have suggested that for limited English proficient students, primary language instruction should be carried out for as much as 70 percent of the school day in early grades (Legaretta-Marcaida, 1981), with English taught as a second language. As children master English, content instruction in English can be increased. A ratio of 50–50, English and other language, through sixth grade sets the stage for additive bilingualism, which opens the door to academic achievement.

Given the obvious constraints of a school day, how is it possible to deliver instruction in two languages across the curriculum? Several methods have been proposed.

### Separation of Languages

Languages may be separated by time, in alternate-day or half-day formats. In a team-teaching situation or when a teacher works with an aide, languages may be separated by person, with each person using one language exclusively. Languages may be separated by place, with rooms or classroom areas designated for particular languages. Languages may also be separated by subject. Some disadvantages of language separation are the following:

- Despite early orthodoxy to the contrary, there is little evidence that language separation has positive effects in the classroom.
- When languages are separated by subject, the ethnic or minority language is often used for areas such as social studies and art, with science and mathematics reserved for English. This is language stereotyping, which damages the prestige of the minority language.
- Likewise, when languages are assigned by person, it is often the teacher's aide who speaks the minority language. Although skilled aides play a necessary and important role in dual language classrooms, a scenario where authority figures in a school speak only English whereas subordinates model minority language proficiency damages minority language prestige.

### Concurrent Translation

Commonly used but not well understood, concurrent translation involves using two languages interchangeably during instruction. There have been several criticisms of this approach.

- Teachers often code-switch, assuming that they are engaged in concurrent translation. While code-switching is linguistically coherent, it is pedagogically random—that is, the switches a bilingual speaker may make in ordinary conversation do not necessarily meet instructional objectives for language development or delivery of content.

- In practice, concurrent translation often approximates direct translation; students quickly learn to tune out the language they don't understand, waiting for the information in the language they do.
- Concurrent translation can be strenuous and tiring for a teacher to implement. Two teachers or a teacher and an aide can implement the method, assuming the availability of sufficient staffing.
- Teachers often overestimate the amount of time spent using the children's primary language and, in fact, spend a disproportionate amount of time speaking English.

The New Concurrent Approach (NCA), developed by Rodolfo Jacobson (1987), suggests using a structured form of code-switching for delivery of content instruction. In Jacobson's method, language switches are carefully planned. There are no intrasentential switches, and all switches are made at the completion of a thought group. Planned switches are justifiable for:

- conceptual reinforcement and review, to assure that all children have mastered the lesson material
- lexical enrichment, to give children the vocabulary necessary to discuss a particular subject in both languages
- appropriateness for curriculum—that is, treating ethnically related events or subjects in the appropriate language

### Preview-Review

The preview-review approach incorporates elements of NCA. In preview-review, content areas are previewed in one language, presented in the other, and reviewed in the first. This method may be particularly useful at the upper primary and secondary levels, where content materials such as science or social studies textbooks may not be readily available in minority languages.

Note that concurrent and preview-review approaches are appropriate for content instruction. Language development in either language and second language instruction should be delivered in the target language.

### COOPERATIVE LEARNING

Cooperative learning is a classroom management strategy that departs from traditional whole-class instructional formats and opens up opportunities for first and second language development. In cooperative learning, the class is divided into teams, whose members work together and rely on one another to learn concepts, solve problems, and complete projects (Kagan, 1986).

A cooperative strategy may be as simple as peer tutoring, where students assist each other with drills and practice for material such as spelling words or math facts. Or cooperative learning can involve teamwork to complete complex projects that require planning, research, and implementation.

There are more chances for students to communicate in a cooperative format than in traditional settings. In addition, the quality of communication is higher as students try to negotiate content-related meaning (Kagan, 1986; Long & Porter, 1985), because cooperative learning creates two-way tasks where each participant has information that the others need.

Cooperative learning models provide rich communication opportunities for limited English proficient students. For example, *Finding Out/Descubrimiento* (DeAvila et al., 1987) uses science and math content to teach critical thinking skills. Students are assigned to task groups with rotating roles such as facilitator, safety officer, and reporter. Groups work on problems in learning centers in areas such as optics, electricity, and water. Materials are provided in English and Spanish, with bilingual students serving as translators. Students can complete their activities working in either language.

Cooperative learning strategies do not involve explicit manipulation of language. Primary language use is permitted in cooperative grouping, but the strategy seems to promote acquisition of the dominant language—English. In that sense, cooperative learning strategies might be classified as a second language teaching approach. It is clear, however, that cooperative strategies produce more opportunities for content-related communication among students than a traditional, teacher-centered classroom environment. Thus they enhance academic learning. In addition, cooperative strategies motivate students and promote a positive affective climate. These qualities make cooperative learning particularly appropriate for a dual language classroom.

## SUMMARY

Program research provides evidence of the value of primary language instruction for language minority students, but is inconclusive. Basic research on bilingualism, however, provides strong support for the value of additive bilingualism. Primary language instruction is justifiable for the following reasons.

- Concepts and skills learned in one language transfer to another.
- Primary language development facilitates second language acquisition.
- Students need time to develop cognitive academic language proficiency.
- Proficiency in two languages has positive effects on achievement.
- Primary language instruction enhances self-concept.

Primary language instruction can be offered in a variety of formats including:

- separation of languages by person, place, time, or subject
- concurrent translation

- preview-review
- cooperative learning strategies

## ACTIVITIES AND QUESTIONS TO THINK ABOUT

1. Visit a classroom within a dual language instructional program. What language strategy does the teacher use in content areas? How does that fit the program model?
2. Monitor language use in the classroom during the period of observation:
   - What percentage of time is each language in use?
   - What are the purposes for which each language is used? Which language is used for instruction in each area? What language is used for reinforcement and praise? for discipline? for instructions?
   - Are language switches purposeful? What purposes can you discern?
   - Are bulletin boards and other classroom displays bilingual?
   - Are materials available in both languages? Are the materials comparable in quantity and quality?
   - Which of the instructors and assistants use which language? How proficient are the personnel in the classroom languages?
   - Overall, are languages assigned equal value in this classroom?
3. Develop an instructional unit in social studies, science, or mathematics that utilizes cooperative learning strategies.

## SUGGESTIONS FOR FURTHER READING

Cummins, J. (1994). Primary language instruction and the education of language minority students. In California State Department of Education (Ed.), *Schooling and language minority students: A theoretical framework* (2nd ed.) (pp. 3–46). Los Angeles: Evaluation, Dissemination, and Assessment Center, California State University, Los Angeles.
Cummins's article sets forth a theoretical framework with an analysis of supporting research that provides a rationale for providing primary language instruction for limited English proficient students. This article, along with others in this new edition, also explores the social, political, and cultural dynamics of schooling for language minority students.

Gonzalez, A., & Guerrero, M. (1983). *A cooperative/interdependent approach to bilingual education.* Hollister, CA: Hollister School District.
This handbook provides detailed practical information about the jigsaw method of cooperative learning. Sample lessons, time lines, and record-keeping forms assist teachers in implementing the jigsaw process in their classrooms.

Kagan, S. (1986). Cooperative learning and sociocultural factors in schooling. In California State Department of Education (Ed.), *Beyond language: Social and cultural factors in schooling language minority students* (pp. 231–298). Los Angeles: Evaluation, Dissemination and Assessment Center, California State University, Los Angeles.
A comprehensive introduction to cooperative learning strategies, this article overviews research results of cooperative learning with special attention to the outcomes of cooperative learning strategies for minority students. The article is particularly useful because it contains an overview of training models and resources available for teachers and schools.

# chapter 7

# Second Language Instruction

The term *English as a Second Language (ESL)* often evokes images on a continuum—ranging from a program separate from a dual language instructional model, involving high-intensity English training, to minimal "pull-out" instruction where limited English proficient children are taken out of their classroom to receive ESL instruction for a small portion of the school day.

Some people erroneously assume that there is a distinct difference between second language instruction and bilingual instruction. Second language instruction, however, is an integrated part of any dual language instructional model. Most dual language instructional programs target limited English proficient students and have an ESL component. There are now, however, programs that include monolingual English speakers, providing an opportunity for them to learn a second language as well.

Language development is basic to schooling, and, as we have already seen, first and second language development can take place in the context of many models. Apart from language development through content instruction, approaches have been developed that focus on second language instruction *per se*. Specific second language methodologies will not be addressed in detail in this chapter, since that is more appropriate to a methods text. This chapter will briefly review traditional and innovative language teaching approaches.

## A NOTE ABOUT TERMINOLOGY

Literature about language instruction sometimes refers to *foreign language instruction*, such as English as a Foreign Language (EFL), and sometimes refers to *second language instruction*, as in English as a Second Language (ESL).

Instructors generally use the term *second language* when it is a language widely used in the immediate social environment. A *foreign* language is one that the student is not likely to encounter in the social environment outside the classroom.

For purposes of dual language instruction it is convenient and logical to refer to *second language instruction*. Programs in the United States are generally geared to teach English to students with limited proficiency in that language. English is clearly a dominant language in the United States and is available in the general social environment. Many programs have two-way goals as well, intending either to restore ethnic languages to children whose families have lost them or to give children in general the opportunity to acquire a new language. Usually the languages offered are present to some extent in the United States, which is a multilingual environment. These languages can therefore be referred to as *second languages*.

Literature that refers to teaching EFL has information that is relevant and applicable to second language instruction. Regardless of the source of information, we will use *second language instruction* as an inclusive term.

## EARLY VIEWPOINTS ON SECOND LANGUAGE INSTRUCTION

### Grammar-Translation

People often claim, "I studied French (or Spanish, or German) for years in school, but I can't speak a word." Many of those people were probably instructed with the grammar-translation method, which focuses on learning language rules and working with written texts. Never apparently very successful, the grammar-translation method is a remnant of the study of Latin grammar, which was highly valued in the Middle Ages. Medieval scholars, however, pursued the intricacies of Latin grammar for its own sake, not necessarily to gain proficiency in the use of Latin. It is likely that skills they gained in day-to-day Latin through direct contact with the language in communicative situations.

As the use of Latin as a vehicle for everyday conversation declined, Latin texts were increasingly translated into vernaculars. The prestige, however, attached to the study of Latin and Greek persisted, as did the idea that the development of grammar skills transferred to other areas of thinking. Resistance to formal study of modern foreign languages continued until well into the eighteenth century, and the grammar-translation approach prevailed despite attempts to devise alternatives (Grittner, 1969).

### The Search for Alternative Approaches

Diller (1978) tells the fascinating story of Francois Gouin, a nineteenth-century Latin teacher from France, who decided to teach himself German. Gouin began by memorizing a German grammar book and 248 irregular verbs, an effort that took him 10 days. Despite these efforts, he was unable to understand a word of spoken German. Convinced, however, that he was on the right track and only needed to broaden his knowledge, he set about memorizing 800 German roots.

At that point, unable to engage in even simple conversation or to translate written German, he purchased a dictionary and proceeded to memorize 30,000 words in 30 days, an effort that all but destroyed his eyesight but failed to make him proficient in German.

Imagine his surprise to find that his three-year-old nephew had learned to speak French during a three-month vacation in France! Focusing his attention on his nephew's accomplishments, Gouin developed the *Series Method,* which involves learning a new language through ordered series of concepts that introduce new vocabulary and grammatical patterns.

Gouin's method was devised on the basis of limited information about language learning, since he focused exclusively on his nephew and never investigated children's language development strategies further. However, his insights about the need to provide real context for language teaching were brilliant, and his early efforts certainly demonstrate the lengths to which people have gone to master a new language.

Another nineteenth-century language instructor, Maximilian Berlitz, literally stumbled on his approach. Berlitz ran a small language school in Providence, Rhode Island. Incapacitated by illness, he hired a French instructor through the mail to assist him. It was only when the instructor arrived in Providence that Berlitz discovered that his new employee spoke only French. With no alternative, he sent the Frenchman off to do the best he could.

When he was sufficiently recovered to visit his school, Berlitz was astonished to discover his students happily conversing in French with far more skill than they had ever acquired before. Based on that revelation, Berlitz developed the *Direct Method,* an approach that immerses students in the second language (Simon, 1980). In the Direct Method, the student's first language is not allowed in the classroom. Materials are presented through a variety of media in an orderly progression, and grammar rules are taught inductively. Although Berlitz gets surprisingly little mention in scholarly discussions of second language instruction, he is a pioneer in immersion methods, and large numbers of students are enrolled in Berlitz schools around the world today.

Late nineteenth- and early twentieth-century attempts to replace grammar-translation with more effective means of second language instruction generally failed to gain popularity. The grammar-translation approach held sway until the onset of World War II.

## MODERN APPROACHES TO SECOND LANGUAGE INSTRUCTION

### The Audiolingual Approach

World War II raised public awareness about the inadequacies of language teaching in the United States. Faced with a pressing need for personnel with skills in many languages, some of which had never been studied or codified, the U.S.

Army developed a revolutionary approach to second language instruction that was called the *audiolingual method.*

The audiolingual approach is based on the assumption that language development requires habit formation and reinforcement. It involves students in language activities that include three components:

- practice and memorization of situation-based dialogues
- drills to reinforce the major patterns in the dialogues
- conversation with a native speaker about the topic of the dialogue

The audiolingual approach was successful and caught on rapidly with some modifications. Some deviations from the original format enhanced the methodology. For example, the original program focused exclusively on the development of oral skills. Teachers quickly found that written materials were useful —especially for adult learners, who had often invented their own writing systems as an aid to memorization.

On the other hand, audiolingual approaches are sometimes implemented using the dialogue and drill components while eliminating the conversation component of the original. In view of recent findings about second language acquisition, it may well be that the real communicative situations were an essential and productive aspect of the army's method.

## Other Recent Approaches

New directions in thinking about second language acquisition unleashed by Chomsky (see Chapter 3), along with dissatisfaction about the state of language instruction, have led to the development of many new approaches to second language instruction. In general, second language instruction has moved away from the tight restrictions inherent in the audiolingual approach and now tends to focus more on the active involvement of students in the language acquisition process.

Modern approaches reflect the idea that language acquisition is a natural and creative process that involves the student in thinking in the new language. Production of the new language arises naturally when a student is ready to begin to speak. Several new approaches have caught the attention of dual and second language instructors. Some may be surprising, since they represent a departure from the language teaching most of us have experienced. These approaches focus on providing language instruction in nonthreatening environments and emphasize communication rather than correct form or knowledge of rules. The following brief descriptions will provide a flavor of recent innovative approaches to second language instruction.

*Total Physical Response (TPR).*   Developed by James Asher, TPR is based on the assumption that a second language is internalized through a process of codebreaking similar to first language development and that the process allows for a long period of listening and developing comprehension prior to production.

Students are given a period of several weeks or months during which they are not asked to produce language and need only respond to commands that require physical movement (Asher, 1982).

***Suggestopedia.***    Developed by Georgi Lozanov, Suggestopedia relies on the assumption that it is possible to increase our ability to learn language by tapping the paraconscious reserves of the brain. Lozanov's method provides a rich acquisition environment; careful attention is paid to the affective dimension of language acquisition. Lessons take place in a pleasant and informal setting.

The culminating component of each Suggestopedia session is unique. Instructors, trained in psychology and art, read language selections in careful synchronization with musical selections. Students prepare for the session by engaging in relaxation techniques derived from yogic meditation and breathing exercises. These exercises activate the subconscious mind and allow students to tap reserves of super memory (Lozanov, 1982).

While many aspects of Suggestopedia would be difficult to implement in the public school setting, innovative aspects of this approach have been incorporated into second language teaching programs with excellent results (Bancroft, 1978).

***Counseling-Learning.***    Developed by Charles Curran (1982), the Counseling-Learning approach is actually an instructional theory that is applicable to a wide variety of subjects. The approach suggests that basic precepts of counseling are broadly applicable to all learning situations. Curran chose to apply his thinking to language teaching since it appeared to be an area where many techniques were unsuccessful. In addition, language teaching is a fruitful area for research, since gains can be readily tested.

Counseling-Learning assumes that there are parallels between a counseling situation and an instructional situation. The learner, or "client," may feel threatened and insecure and may experience conflict and frustration. The role of the teacher or "counselor" is to empathize with the student (client) and to provide the learner with skills that will eliminate frustration. Students work in small groups and initiate conversations in their native languages, which are then translated by language experts who sit outside the circle. As students become less anxious and more proficient, conversations become more personal and more linguistically complex, and students require less assistance from the experts. Tape recordings of the sessions and brief sessions on points of grammar provide opportunities for review and clarification.

Curran's research indicates that students who attempted new languages with the counseling method made favorable progress when compared with students who participated in traditional college language classes (Curran, 1982).

***The Notional-Functional Approach.***    While TPR, Suggestopedia, and Counseling-Learning have been called *interpersonal* approaches (Brown, 1980), reflecting a strong concern for the importance of the affective variable in second language learning, the notional-functional approach considers the pragmatics of language. A notional-functional syllabus organizes instruction around the functions of language. Students learn appropriate communication strategies for a variety of situations. For example, a notional-functional syllabus might provide students with opportunities to learn to agree, argue, question, or compliment.

***The Natural Approach.***    Stephen Krashen's theory of language acquisition (see Chapter 4) inspired the development of the Natural Approach (Krashen & Terrell, 1983) to second language teaching. The Natural Approach is of particular interest to instructors at the primary level, since it has greater practical applicability at the elementary level than many of the other new communication-based approaches, such as Suggestopedia. We will, therefore, outline the Natural Approach in some detail.

According to Krashen, language acquisition will occur when certain conditions are met. The Natural Approach (Terrell, 1981) meets those conditions by:

- providing comprehensible input
- focusing on communication of messages
- creating low-anxiety situations

The Natural Approach assumes that speech emerges in four natural and distinct stages:

1. *preproduction,* when students communicate primarily with gesture and actions
2. *early production,* when students begin to use one- or two-word utterances, or short phrases
3. *speech emergence,* when students use longer phrases or complete sentences
4. *intermediate fluency,* when students can engage in conversation and produce connected narratives

Instruction in the Natural Approach is organized according to these progressive levels of language acquisition. At the outset the teacher supplies a lot of comprehensible input, but does not demand production from the students. As students progress, the teacher introduces new receptive vocabulary and encourages higher levels of language use. Reading and writing activities are incorporated into the curriculum when students have reached intermediate fluency.

The Natural Approach promotes basic proficiency and is particularly appropriate for primary levels. However, overreliance on approaches that do not explicitly address syntax may result in fossilization or the internalization of incorrect forms. As students advance in their second language, therefore, teachers generally supplement the Natural Approach with instruction in language arts areas such as reading, writing, and critical thinking.

## INTEGRATING LANGUAGE AND CONTENT: SPECIALLY DESIGNED ACADEMIC INSTRUCTION IN ENGLISH

Recently, educators have begun to understand that language learning is most meaningful when it is tied to content instruction. Snow, Met, and Genesee (1989) suggest that language development is facilitated when it is combined with content area instruction for the following reasons:

- Cognitive development and language development are inextricably tied, especially for young children.
- School subjects are what children need to talk about in school, so content area provides both the motivation and the opportunity for meaningful communication.
- Tying language development to content area allows students to develop the kind of language that is used in school. (See Chapter 6 for a discussion of Cognitive Academic Language Proficiency.)

Increasingly, teachers are utilizing an approach called *Specially Designed Academic Instruction in English (SDAIE)* to assist second language learners in developing their abilities in English while they master the concepts and skills in the required curriculum.

SDAIE is particularly useful in situations that arise where primary language instruction is difficult or impossible—for example:

- bilingual staff is unavailable to meet all students' needs, and/or
- the classroom contains students with a variety of primary languages other than English.

In general, SDAIE combines the important components of quality teaching with approaches based on second language acquisition theory. Properly implemented, SDAIE addresses all areas of instruction, including planning, classroom management, lesson delivery, and assessment.

## Planning

In SDAIE, language is seen as the vehicle for content, and vice versa. Consequently, teachers plan each lesson not only to meet the curricular objectives related to content but also to include appropriate language objectives. Met (1994) distinguishes between content-obligatory and content-compatible language objectives. *Content-obligatory objectives* are those that must be included to make a lesson comprehensible for students. So, for example, second language learners studying the Civil War need to be familiar with words like *enslavement, federalism,* and *emancipation.*

*Content-compatible objectives* are those that can be tied into the subject matter to assist students in language growth and development but aren't mandatory for students to understand the subject at hand. In the case of the Civil War, a teacher could, for example, emphasize the use of conditional phrases: "What would have happened if John Wilkes Booth had failed to assassinate the president?" Use of the conditional can be incorporated into almost any subject area and isn't required for students to learn about the Civil War. Based on an assessment of students' language development and needs, however, a teacher might want to include this content-compatible objective.

## Classroom Management

Classroom management is an important component of SDAIE. If we accept current analyses of the ways that students develop in their second language, we can assume that we need to provide safe, comfortable classroom environments and organize instruction to provide opportunities for students to interact around meaningful activities. Cooperative grouping, described in Chapter 6, is one useful approach. Buddy systems and peer-tutoring systems also allow students to try out their language in a nonthreatening environment while completing academic tasks.

## Lesson Delivery

***Sheltered English.***   One important methodology within SDAIE is sheltered English. In a sheltered classroom, English is used as the medium of instruction in the content areas, and teachers use strategies to encourage English acquisition through comprehensible input and contextualization. Such strategies might include:

- slow but natural levels of speech
- clear enunciation
- short, simple sentences
- repetition and paraphrasing
- controlled vocabulary and idioms
- visual reinforcement through the use of gestures, props, pictures, films, demonstrations, and hands-on activities
- frequent comprehension checks

Teachers in a sheltered English classroom maintain a setting with a low level of anxiety, stressing comprehension prior to eliciting production and emphasizing communication over correctness. Activities are selected that encourage hands-on, active engagement with the material, as well as social interaction among students.

Thematic instruction has particular utility in sheltered classrooms because students encounter familiar language across several subject areas. Thematic instruction has been defined as "a learning sequence defined around a theme or topic offering students opportunities to use oral language, reading, writing, and critical thinking for learning and sharing ideas" (Peregoy & Boyle, 1993, p. 40). One teacher in Santa Clara County, California, organizes each school year around a single theme. In 1993, for a combination fifth/sixth/seventh-grade class, the central theme for the school year was titled "Kokopelli's Flute—A Song of the Southwest" (Perssons, 1993). The school year started with "Story of the Earth," in which students read, illustrated, and dramatized ancient myths, and culminated with a field trip to the Southwest, organized in great measure by the students themselves.

Students in sheltered settings should have an intermediate command of English and should be grouped within the classroom according to their English ability. It is important to remember, however, that it is not the objective of a sheltered classroom to provide remediation in subject areas. The subject content and objectives of a sheltered classroom should be identical to those of a mainstream classroom in the same subject.

***Cognitive Academic Language Learning Approach (CALLA).*** First developed by Chamot and O'Malley (1987), CALLA is an approach designed to assist students who are making the transition from bilingual to mainstream classrooms. CALLA originally focused on mathematics, science, and social studies, and has been expanded to incorporate literature and language arts (1994). In CALLA, second language learners are taught to manage and monitor their own language and content learning. CALLA explicitly teaches learners to:

- plan for learning, using metacognitive strategies such as skimming a text to identify the main organizing concept;
- engage the material, using cognitive strategies such as note-taking and summarizing; and
- interact socially, using social affective learning strategies, such as asking clarifying questions or working with another student (Chamot & O'Malley, 1994).

## Assessment

Assessment is a key part of any instructional approach. Genesee and Hamayan (1994) point out that when language instruction is integrated with content instruction, teachers need to use a variety of assessment techniques that distinguish between students' language abilities and growth and their mastery of subject matter.

Standardized testing has traditionally been the backbone of classroom assessment of student achievement, but teachers are turning increasingly to what have been called *alternative assessment approaches.* One form of alternative assessment is performance assessment. In performance assessment, "a student completes an assignment alone or with other students, often in a content area, and prepares a summary or interpretation of the activity. . . ." (O'Malley & Valdez Pierce, 1991, p. 2) which is then evaluated by the teacher. Many teachers are now combining the results of traditional and alternative assessments into portfolios.

Portfolios allow students to present work in their native language or in ways that are not exclusively language bound, such as photographs and videos. They also allow students to observe their progress in language development over time. Portfolios also allow parents of second language learners to see what their children are doing in school (Genesee & Hamayan, 1994; O'Malley & Valdez Pierce, 1992).

## LITERACY AND BILITERACY

### What Is Literacy?

A student entering high school from eighth grade expressed surprise to me that he had to take a class in English.

"Why do I have to take English in high school?" he said. "I speak it already!"

"Because you've got to read Shakespeare, and where else will you do it if not in high school?!" I replied.

My reply was only half-joking: As a modern, literate society, we share the assumptions—correct but usually unexplored—that language development continues through adolescence and young adulthood and that full language development includes literacy. Consequently, we require English speakers to take English in high school and through college.

In other words, literacy means more to us than simply mastering the ability to decode the written word. As one author puts it, "Literacy can be viewed . . . as the ability to think and reason like a literate person, *within a particular society*" (Langer, 1991, p. 11).

Furthermore, literacy has political implications. Since the earliest times of our republic, literacy has been seen as the key to participation in a representative democracy. In a literate society, the ability to read is the key that unlocks the doors to the knowledge base of the culture of power and to the political system. Williams and Capizzi Snipper define *critical literacy* as the ability to determine "what effect a writer is attempting to bring about in readers, why he or she is making the effort, and just who those readers are" (1990, p. 11). In common parlance, a critical reader can read between the lines. It is not surprising, therefore, that the most repressive regimes in the world are the ones that offer the least opportunity for schooling or support for literacy.

### Biliteracy

Often, when people discuss bilingualism and bilingual education, their attention is focused on the ability to speak a language. A preservice student teacher in a class on bilingualism once asked, "If children come from Spanish-speaking families, why do they need to study Spanish in school? Won't they learn it at home?" Children in Spanish-speaking households learn Spanish just like children in English-speaking households learn English.

But much as we assume that English speakers will develop literacy in their language in school, so speakers of other languages benefit from the language development that a school setting offers. And much as we expect an English speaker to be familiar with the great works of English language literature (abbreviated as "Shakespeare" in my reply to the eighth grader), or to write research papers and business letters in an appropriate format, so an educated Spanish speaker needs formal instruction to perform comparably in Spanish. Biliteracy, then, includes the development of the full range of understanding and skills appropriate for an educated speaker of two languages.

## How Can Teachers Support Biliteracy?

Theoretically, literacy is most readily achieved in a student's first language. Note that this generalization may not apply in American schools to speakers of some Asian languages such as Chinese. Mastery of the Chinese writing system is arduous, and youngsters may more readily learn to read in English, assuming that they have acquired some oral proficiency.

In general, however, as we have already seen, most of the concepts and skills that support our ability to read transfer readily from one language to another. Once we are literate in any language, we are literate. While we need to learn specific features of a new writing system, we don't need to learn to read each time we learn to read a new language.

## Literacy and the Second Language Learner

The process of becoming literate involves the construction and creation of meaning through text. Current theorists suggest this interaction with text to engage meaning is both cognitive and social (Hudelson, 1994; Riggs 1991). Citing Goodman and Goodman, Riggs asserts that "in a literate society, using written language is as natural as using conversation, and the uses of written language develop as naturally as do the uses of oral language" (1991, p. 524).

Many of the strategies that teachers use to develop native literacy are useful for assisting students to develop literacy in a new language. Hudelson (1994) suggests that teachers create a print-rich environment, provide opportunities for collaboration, and organize instruction so that students engage literature in a meaningful way and write purposefully.

It is important to remember, however, that text is embedded in cultural and social contexts, which may be unfamiliar to second language learners. Escamilla (1993) points out that students can answer many conventionally structured comprehension questions by quoting directly from a text without any real understanding. Harman (1991) provides an excellent example of how this is possible with a nonsense sample text: "The three blugy chinzles slotted prusily on the flubbish werlies." By referring to the text, it is possible to answer the question

"How did the blugy chinzles slottle?" (p. 144) without any real comprehension. Teachers of second language learners need to develop strategies for evaluating whether students have engaged the real meaning of a text.

## How Can Schools Promote Biliteracy?

In the American context, the development of fully bilingual and biliterate students requires a rethinking of language education. First, we must promote maintenance bilingual education for language minority students and enrichment language instruction for native English speakers. Then we must extend our programming to include secondary and post-secondary education. For example, all too often, native Spanish speakers have little opportunity to develop skills in reading and writing Spanish. Courses specifically geared for native speakers are offered at some high schools and colleges, but they are still relatively rare. Expansion of our efforts will no doubt require that educators promote understanding of the dimensions and value of biliteracy.

## SUMMARY

Dual language instructional programs include a component for developing students' proficiency in a second language. Grammar-translation approaches have dominated second language instruction for centuries, despite their ineffectuality in developing communicative competence. The audiolingual approach, first developed for military purposes, relies heavily on habit formation and has proven somewhat useful.

Theories about second language acquisition have led to the development of approaches that attempt to develop communicative competence. Total Physical Response, Suggestopedia, and Counseling-Learning pay careful attention to the need to address the affective variables in second language learning. Notional-functional approaches respond to the pragmatics of language and organize activities around language functions.

Krashen's theory of second language acquisition has formed the basis for the Natural Approach, which attempts to provide rich, comprehensible input to students in a comfortable environment as they move through the stages of language development.

Specially Designed Academic Instruction in English (SDAIE) combines second language instruction with content instruction. SDAIE applies to all aspects of instruction, including planning, classroom management, lesson delivery, and assessment. It is useful for intermediate second language speakers and as a bridge for students about to make the transition to all-English classrooms.

Literacy and biliteracy are important considerations in dual language instruction. Literacy must be defined as *critical literacy,* and students should have the opportunity to develop their critical literacy skills to the fullest extent in both their languages.

## ACTIVITIES AND QUESTIONS TO THINK ABOUT

1. Visit a primary level and a secondary/adult second language lesson. What kind of assumptions underlie the kind of approach in use? To what extent are these assumptions in keeping with current second language acquisition theory?

2. Investigate commercial language teaching programs in your area. What languages are taught? What approaches are used? How much do the course(s) or program(s) cost? How many students are enrolled in the program(s)?

3. Develop a lesson plan in social studies, science, or mathematics appropriate for a sheltered English setting. Include content-obligatory and content-compatible language objectives. Describe how you plan to contextualize the material. Be careful to maintain the level of the material in the lesson while modifying the delivery for intermediate second language learners. Include an assessment component.

## SUGGESTIONS FOR FURTHER READING

Asher, J. (1986). *Learning another language through actions. The complete teacher's guidebook.* Los Gatos, CA: Sky Oaks Productions.
A handbook on Total Physical Response, this book provides background on how the approach was developed, documents its effectiveness, answers common questions about it, and provides a lesson-by-lesson plan for its implementation.

Blair, R. W. (Ed.). (1982). *Innovative approaches to language teaching.* Rowley, MA: Newbury House.
Blair divides language teaching approaches into three categories: the comprehension approach, approaches to a rich acquisition environment, and rich learning environment approaches. Within those categories, the book contains articles by a number of authors, including Asher, Terrell, and Lozanov. The introduction to the book sets the development of language teaching in a historical context and also contains a paper presented by Krashen at Brigham Young University in 1979 that is an excellent introduction to his theories on language acquisition. The book's bibliography is particularly useful because it contains references divided by teaching approaches.

Freeman, D. E., & Freeman, Y. S. (1994). *Between worlds: Access to second language acquisition.* Portsmouth, NH: Heinemann.
Combining descriptions of theory with practice and examples of student work, this book is useful to all teachers who want to support their second language learners. The book is particularly valuable because it speaks to the cultural and social contexts of second language learning and reaches beyond the classroom, showing teachers how to work with their students' families and communities. Appendixes include bibliographies related to second language acquisiton theory, methods of teaching, and resources for classroom use.

Hamayan, E. V., & Perlman, R. (1990, Spring). *Helping language minority students after they exit from bilingual/ESL programs: A handbook for teachers.* Rosslyn, VA: National Clearinghouse for Bilingual Education.
This short publication enumerates and explains strategies that teachers can use to shelter their content-area instruction to assist their second language learners. The handbook provides detailed information about setting up and monitoring a buddy system that pairs second language learners with bilingual or monolingual English speaking students.

Krashen, S. D., & Terrell, T. D. (1983). *The Natural Approach: Language acquisition in the classroom.* San Francisco: The Alemany Press.

This book contains an explanation of Krashen's theory of language acquisition and develops the implications of the theory for classroom instruction. Several chapters are devoted to actual classroom activities for the implementation of the Natural Approach. The introductory chapter provides a historical overview of second language instruction, which provides the context for the development of this new approach.

Peregoy, S. F., & Boyle, O. F. (1993). *Reading, writing, and learning in ESL: A resource book for K–8 teachers.* White Plains, NY: Longman.

Clear direction for teaching reading and writing in English to English as a second language learners, this book includes activities and resources, and addresses the daily concerns of classroom teachers.

Pérez, B., & Torres-Guzmán, M. (1992). *Learning in two worlds: An integrated Spanish/ English biliteracy approach.* White Plains, NY: Longman.

Specific strategies, illustrated liberally with samples of children's work, make this a useful guide for the teacher who wants to implement a literacy program within the context of a dual language instructional model.

Ramírez, A. G. (1995). *Creating contexts for second language acquisition: Theory and methods.* White Plains, NY: Longman.

This book is comprehensive, up to date, and useful. It includes a well-organized overview of current theory as well as useful directions for practice, with descriptions and examples of ways to teach listening, speaking, reading, and writing to second language learners. The book deserves special acknowledgement for attention to the dynamics of culture in second language learning.

Richard-Amato, P. A. (1988). *Making it happen: Interaction in the second language classroom from theory to practice.* White Plains, NY: Longman.

A collection of methods and activities for second language teaching, this book focuses on the importance of interaction in second language instruction. The last section of the book includes several excellent readings that provide background on second language acquisition theories.

Richard-Amato, P. A., & Snow, M. A. (1992). *The multicultural classroom: Readings for content-area teachers.* White Plains, NY: Longman.

Following a collection of articles that define a theoretical framework and describe cultural considerations, this book addresses itself to the specifics of classroom instruction in social studies, mathematics, science, art, physical education, music, and literacy development for second language learners.

# chapter **8**

# Aspects of Culture

Language and its use in the classroom are natural foci for the study of dual language instruction. Language, however, is inextricably bound with culture, and cultural factors have an important influence on educational outcomes for all students.

The history of the United States has always been characterized by cultural diversity, but never so much as in modern times. The last part of the twentieth century has seen unprecedented numbers of immigrants coming to the United States. In addition, changes in immigration law in 1965 have opened the door to newcomers from every corner of the world.

Nowhere is the impact of continued and varied immigration felt more than in the public schools. Each day, teachers attempt to meet the needs of children from many different cultural backgrounds. This chapter will attempt to clarify definitions of culture and provide examples of its characteristics and manifestations.

## CULTURE AND POPULATION

American culture is difficult to characterize because it is made up of many complex and changing subcultures. In fact, complexity and change are at the heart of American culture. The demographics of the United States are in flux at the current time for a variety of reasons.

### The Impact of Immigration

Compelled by war or famine or lured by the prospect of life in a new and exciting world, people have been immigrating to the New World since before the inception of the United States as a nation. In the nineteenth century, social, political, and economic upheaval caused an influx of people from all over Europe. The Irish arrived, having fled the potato famines. German and Scandinavian farmers were attracted by the farmlands of the Midwest. Chinese laborers built our transcontinental railroad lines. Italians, Poles, and Czechs, attracted by the opportunities for economic success and freedom from oppression, all made their way to United States in the late 1800s.

The nineteenth-century wave of immigration swelled into the twentieth, reaching a peak between 1900 and 1920, when numbers of Italians and Eastern European Jews flooded East Coast ports and Mexicans, displaced by the Revolution of 1910, immigrated northward to the Southwest and California.

Reaction to newcomers was swift and often vicious. Xenophobia (a fear of things that seem foreign) and racism led to attempts to limit immigration. The Chinese Exclusion Act of 1882 was the first federal attempt to limit immigration by nationality. The 1917 Immigration Act excluded Asians, and the National Origins Act of 1924 established quotas for nations outside the Western Hemisphere (The Immigration Project, 1981).

In 1965, however, President Lyndon B. Johnson signed legislation that altered national immigration policy. Prior to 1965, immigration law favored ethnic groups who were already represented in the U.S. population. Johnson's legislation placed an annual limit of 20,000 immigrants for each country. As a result, people are entering the United States in significant numbers from all over the world. In 1984 the United States admitted 600,000 legal immigrants.

Official numbers do not appear to exceed figures of the early part of the century, but illegal immigration adds significant numbers—perhaps doubling official counts ("Growth of a Nation," 1985). Not only has the number of immigrants increased, but the diversity of newcomers has increased as well, with the flow from Europe decreasing and the influx from Latin America and Asia increasing.

## Other Demographic Factors

While steady and varied immigration has an undeniable and dynamic impact on our profile as a nation, it is not the only factor that affects the demographic picture. Differential rates of growth among various groups also have a significant effect on our population. The "baby boom" that occurred after World War II was primarily a white middle-class phenomenon, and the rate of growth in that segment of the population has since decreased significantly. White women, in general, are expected to produce less than 2 children per lifetime. Black women, however, are currently expected to produce 2.4 children per lifetime, and for Mexican American women the rate is 2.9.

In addition, the population of people of color is younger than the white population. The average age of the white population is about 31 years. The nonwhite population is considerably younger: the median age for blacks is about 25; for Hispanics, just over 22 ("Here They Come," 1986).

The changing demographic and cultural situation in our schools means that all teachers will have to develop skills to work with children who fall into the following categories.

- *Language minority children:* These are children who experience a language other than English spoken in their homes. They may be bilingual or may speak only English. In either case, they are likely to have links to an ethnic minority culture.

- *Limited English proficient children:* These children come from a variety of linguistic and cultural backgrounds and have insufficient skills in English to succeed in an English-only classroom. The federal government estimates indicate that there were approximately 2.3 million limited English proficient children in the United States in 1992 (U.S. Department of Education, 1992). While public school enrollments rose only 4.2 percent between 1986 and 1991, the number of limited English proficient students increased 50 percent (Gray, 1993). California, which enrolls nearly 10 percent of the nation's schoolchildren, identified 1,215,218 limited English proficient students, K-12 in 1994. Across the country, 43 percent of all school districts serve limited English proficient students (Garcia & Figueroa, 1994). Table 8.1 shows the number of limited English proficient students by state for the 1991–92 school year (U.S. Department of Education, 1992).

The school traditionally has been a gateway to mainstream culture for the diverse groups that make up U.S. society. As the population changes, and indeed as our concept of mainstream culture is altered by the groups that enter the United States, teachers will need to develop a deep understanding of the nature of culture and the implications of diversity in the classroom.

## WHAT IS CULTURE?

Like language, our own culture is usually invisible to us. We tend to associate culture with things that are far away and exotic. A student of mine once commented, "I didn't know there was such a thing as American culture until I spent time in Central America." Away from home, amid people who operate under different assumptions, that student was able to perceive characteristics of her own culture. According to an old Japanese saying, "One sees the sky through a hollow reed." If we equate the sky to reality, then the hollow reed through which we view it may be likened to our culture. But what exactly is culture?

Definitions of culture abound in social science literature, and the search for a single definition can be perplexing and frustrating. As basic social science assumptions have changed over time, so have definitions of culture. The trend toward behaviorist thinking gave rise to definitions of culture that

**TABLE 8.1**  Number of Limited English Proficient (LEP) students by state (school year 1991–1992)

| State | Number of LEP Students |
|---|---|
| Alabama | 1,052 |
| Alaska | 11,184 |
| Arkansas | 65,727 |
| Arizona | 2,000 |
| California | 986,462 |
| Colorado | 17,187 |
| Connecticut | 16,988 |
| District of Columbia | 3,379 |
| Delaware | 1,969 |
| Florida | 83,937 |
| Georgia | 6,487 |
| Hawaii | 9,730 |
| Idaho | 3,986 |
| Illinois | 79,291 |
| Indiana | 4,670 |
| Iowa | 3,705 |
| Kansas | 4,661 |
| Kentucky | 1,071 |
| Louisiana | 8,345 |
| Maine | 1,983 |
| Maryland | 12,701 |
| Massachusetts | 42,606 |
| Michigan | 37,112 |
| Minnesota | 13,204 |
| Mississippi | 2,753 |
| Missouri | 3,815 |
| Montana | 6,635 |
| Nebraska | 1,257 |
| Nevada | 9,057 |
| New Hampshire | 1,146 |
| New Jersey | 47,560 |
| New Mexico | 73,505 |
| New York | 168,208 |
| North Carolina | 6,030 |
| North Dakota | 7,187 |
| Ohio | 8,992 |
| Oklahoma | 15,860 |
| Oregon | 7,557 |
| Pennsylvania | 15,000 |
| Rhode Island | 7,632 |
| South Carolina | 1,205 |

**TABLE 8.1**  (continued)

| | |
|---|---|
| South Dakota | 6,691 |
| Tennessee | 3,660 |
| Texas | 313,234 |
| Utah | 14,860 |
| Vermont | 500 |
| Virginia | 15,130 |
| Washington | 28,646 |
| West Virginia | 231 |
| Wisconsin | 14,648 |
| Wyoming | 1,919 |
| Total: | 2,263,682* |

*Total also includes: American Samoa, Canal Zone, Guam, Puerto Rico, Trust Territories, and Virgin Islands
SOURCE:   U.S. Department of Education, Office of the Secretary. (1992). *The condition of bilingual education in the nation: A report to Congress and the President, June 30, 1992.* Washington, DC: U.S. Government Printing Office.

emphasized a particular group's observable patterns of behavior. In the 1950s, the thinking of cognitive psychologists influenced anthropologists, who began to conceptualize culture in terms of ideas and beliefs to the exclusion of observable behaviors.

One frequently cited definition describes culture as a system of standards for perceiving, believing, evaluating, and acting (Goodenough, 1971). Each culture has many complex and overlapping systems within which its members operate and through which they assign and extract meaning. When you encounter a culture different from your own, you try to figure out how things work (cultural behavior) and why they function as they do (cultural knowledge).

For our purposes, it is useful to accept a fairly inclusive approach to the concept of culture. One analysis (Arvizu, Snyder, & Espinosa, 1980) suggests that culture is "a dynamic, creative, and continuous process including behaviors, values, and substance learned and shared by people that guides them in their struggle for survival and gives meaning to their lives." Let us consider the components of this definition—that is, the characteristics of culture.

## Culture Is Dynamic

Just as language changes over time to meet the needs of its users, culture changes over time as people adapt to changing circumstances. For example, people often think of Native Americans as people who live in tepees, wear feather headdresses, and hunt buffalo. That characterization might be historically accurate to a limited extent, but it no longer applies—despite pervasive media images to the contrary. While Native Americans today cherish and protect their traditional heritages, they are also likely to be part of mainstream U.S. culture.

## Culture Is Creative

The process of cultural change is one of creativity. Each new environmental change results in a cultural adaptation. Old ways are replaced by the new in dynamic and creative ways. For example, economic circumstances in the United States have resulted in large numbers of women entering the wage-earning workforce. The result has been a change in our perception of family structure, in our belief system about the abilities of women, and in systems for caring for children outside the immediate family.

## Culture Is Continuous

Changing circumstances produce new systems of action, belief, and perception, but the new systems contain traces of the old. Such traces are what we call *tradition.* Each successive generation passes on its cumulative culture to the next. Chinese Americans, for example, celebrate the Chinese New Year in the United States. While the traditional week-long celebration is impractical in the modern U.S. setting, traditions in foods and customs are still maintained.

## Culture Is Learned

We are not born with our culture. A film called *Living on Tokyo Time* (Okazaki, 1987) tells the story of a young Japanese woman who emigrates to California and marries a Japanese American man in order to obtain legal immigration status. The movie recounts her experience and her surprise as she discovers that, although her new husband looks like someone from Japan, he is unfamiliar with Japanese customs and even with Japanese food. Such characteristics as the color of our hair and eyes are genetically determined, but we learn our culture as we are socialized by the people and circumstances that surround us, in a process called *enculturation.*

## Culture Is Shared

Just as language is useful only if we agree on certain conventions, culture needs shared assumptions in order to function. Some of you, for example, may belong to an in-group or subculture that uses a particular handshake as a greeting. Members of that group rely on the handshake as a symbol for group membership and a way of opening a social interaction. Such a symbol is useful only if members of the group share an understanding of its meaning.

The assumption that culture is shared is operative even when a particular behavior or activity is not. For example, in the United States, people generally brush their teeth individually, in private. Despite the absence of others, each of us usually brushes his or her teeth according to shared culture knowledge about what to use and how to proceed, with certain shared assumptions about the value of dental care.

Every culture is extremely complex, and not every member knows all the systems and symbols involved. Conversely, most of us belong to more than one subculture and may be competent in the symbols and systems of several (Goodenough, 1971).

## Culture Is a Struggle for Survival

Each culture is an adaptive response to a particular environment. The symbols and systems of a culture evolve to allow a particular group to adjust to its circumstances. As mentioned before, we tend to have an inaccurate and stereotypical view of Native Americans, both as they are in the present and as they were in the past. Photographs, however, that Edward S. Curtis took between 1896 and 1930 (Brown, 1972) reveal the astounding number and variety of Native American cultures that existed on the North American continent prior to European domination.

The hunting tribes of the Great Plains lived in tepees, which were made of readily available buffalo skins and easily transported in keeping with the tribe members' needs as nomadic hunters. Indians of the coastal Northwest, on the other hand, lived in reed houses and were skilled as fishermen. Each group developed a culture that met its needs for survival and responded to the resources and demands of its environment.

## CULTURE AND LANGUAGE

The relationship of culture and language has been of interest to anthropologists and linguists since the early twentieth century. The debate centers around Edward Sapir's suggestion that speakers of different languages have different perceptions of the world; that is, that language determines culture. This view, promulgated by his student Benjamin Lee Whorf, is sometimes called the Whorf (or Sapir-Whorf) hypothesis. The layperson's expression of the Whorf hypothesis is often stated in this way: "There are some things you can only say in Spanish" or whatever language the speaker holds dear.

One researcher (Chaika, 1989) has characterized language as "a mirror of its speakers' attitudes and ideas. A mirror reflects. It does not determine; it does not hold prisoners" (p. 295). As we saw in our discussion of the nature of language in Chapter 3, language changes and adapts to meet the needs of its speakers. While some languages may have more concise forms of expression for objects or concepts that exist in a particular culture, any language can express any idea that its culture requires. Rheingold (1988) provides a list of words from different languages for which there are no one-word equivalents in English. The meanings of these words can, however, be expressed in English, as the following definitions show:

- *mamihlapinatapei* (Tierra del Fuegan, noun): a meaningful look, shared by two people, expressing mutual unstated feelings
- *wabi* (Japanese, noun): a flawed detail that creates an elegant whole
- *bricoleur* (French, noun): a person who constructs things by random messing around without following an explicit plan
- *biritilulo* (Kiriwina, New Guinean, noun): comparing yams to settle disputes
- *mbuki-mvuki* (Bantu, verb): to shuck off clothes in order to dance

The debate as to whether or not language determines culture will undoubtedly continue. There is little question, however, that language and culture are inseparable, and learning a new language invariably entails learning a new culture.

In the motion picture *Born in East L.A.* (Marin & Macgregor-Scott, 1987), a native-born Mexican American is mistakenly deported from Los Angeles to Mexico. Trying to earn his way back to the United States, he takes a job with a *coyote* (people smuggler), teaching people English so they can blend in when they make their way across the border. His students are Asian immigrants trying to cross the border into the United States illegally. He quickly discerns what they will need to know in Los Angeles. He dresses them in bandannas, teaches them a "cool" walk, and begins their training in English with the words "*Orale vato,* wha's happenin'!" (Hey buddy, what's happening?) It is clear from the outset that language learning must be accompanied by culture learning.

## HOW IS CULTURE MANIFESTED?

James P. Spradley (1972) commented, "The man in the street is a naive realist who lives in a world he can count on, a world he believes is much the same for everyone else" (p. 8). In other words, we usually assume that the qualities we perceive in the world around us and the meanings we assign to symbols and events are concrete and universal. On the contrary, people around the world have devised an infinite number and variety of social institutions, daily habits, and meaning systems in their quest for survival.

To get a sense of the vastness of the cultural enterprise, we will look at a few of the many manifestations of culture. All of us are familiar with myriad examples of each culture area. Exemplification, however, sometimes leads to stereotyping. The examples presented here are meant to be illustrative but may be somewhat oversimplified.

## Clothing and Decoration

While we might immediately assume that the purpose of clothing is for protection against the weather, a closer look shows us that people use clothing for a variety of purposes such as gender differentiation, status display, and ritual.

For example, if you have ever planned a wedding, you know how much emphasis is placed on proper dress for everyone involved. In middle-class mainstream U.S. culture, brides often wear white, but they may not—depending on the formality of the occasion or their previous marital status. Attendants are carefully dressed, and the groom and his party must be attired in keeping with the nature of the event. Flowers are carefully selected and arranged. Stores even market mother-of-the-bride dresses, indicating that we have a particular cultural expectation of the bride's mother. Rites of passage and other ceremonial events require special dress and adornment that differ from culture to culture.

## Housing

Again, it seems logical to assume that the purpose of housing is protection: as shelter, housing generally conforms to the resources and demands of each particular environment. Stone houses in New England are practical and serviceable in an environment with abundant large rocks in the soil and a cold climate. Such houses would be impractical and out of place near the equator, where the climate is always warm and humid, or for nomadic peoples, who need shelters that can be dismantled and carried for long distances.

But housing, like clothing, serves purposes beyond the need for protection. A home may serve as a center for family or community life, and an analysis of housing often reveals social organization. Houses may also indicate status. For example, the president of the United States always resides in the White House for the duration of the term. While not necessarily the most opulent residence in the country, the White House has social and historical significance.

## Time Orientation

Different cultures have different orientations to time. You may have encountered an overt reference to cultural time orientation if you have been invited to a party and were told that it would start at six o'clock in the evening *hora Latina* (Latin time). Such an invitation acknowledges the fact that in the Hispanic cultural context, a social invitation for six o'clock may indicate an event that will start no earlier than seven in the evening. If you were to appear at six, you would likely be the first to arrive and would find your hosts unprepared. Some people might suggest that Hispanics are not prompt or "have no sense of time." Such an ethnocentric view fails to understand that each of us knows when to arrive for a particular event within the context of our culture or subculture.

## Spatial Orientation

Each culture has its own patterns for the use of personal space. You may have noticed a proxemic pattern if you were born in the United States and have had a conversation with a person born in the Middle East. Middle Easterners and North Americans have different concepts of appropriate distance for nonintimate personal conversation, with the Middle Easterners standing closer to each other than the North Americans do. Such differences often cause misjudgments and misunderstandings; one person assuming that the other is moving in too close while the other person judges the first as aloof or uncaring. Proxemic patterns also manifest themselves in architecture, arrangement of furnishings, and body language (Hall, 1966).

## Values

Each culture has a frame of reference for identifying what is desirable or important to the group. The academic achievement of newly arrived Asian immigrants has led to speculation that their success is related to the Confucian value system and the value it places on scholarship (Butterfield, 1986). Without entering into a discussion of the merits of that suggestion, we note that it acknowledges the role of values in culture.

Although values are harder to identify than the material aspects of culture, they are of particular importance to teachers. All too often, teachers acknowledge surface aspects of culture through ethnic heritage celebrations, classroom decor, and curriculum materials. While such acknowledgements of material or surface culture are worthwhile, they are not sufficient.

For example, it has been said that Navajo children from traditional backgrounds look down when they are addressed by a teacher. Teachers who fail to understand that the children are showing them respect within the context of Navajo culture often misinterpret this behavior and assume that the students are disrespectful or even sneaky. Mainstream American culture places a high value on direct eye contact, as manifested in expressions such as, "I looked him straight in the eye."

One teacher tells of his difficulty in trying to encourage Rosa, a Mexican American high school student in his remedial English class. In an attempt to express a genuine interest in her, he complimented her on a new hairstyle. Shortly thereafter, she began cutting class and finally revealed to a counselor that she thought the teacher was taking an inappropriate romantic interest in her (Wineburg, 1987). In that case, the values difference between Rosa and her teacher led to an uncomfortable and potentially serious misunderstanding. Misunderstanding of deep culture or value systems may result in discriminatory treatment of children from minority groups. Deep or "invisible" culture will be discussed in the following chapter.

## SUMMARY

The demography of the United States is changing significantly, due both to immigration and to differences among ethnic groups in average age and birth rates. Schools are particularly affected by these demographic changes, so that teachers are working increasingly with children from diverse linguistic and cultural backgrounds.

Culture is something we all have but often find difficult to perceive. Culture, like language, is dynamic, changing to meet the needs of the people it serves. All cultures have coherent, shared systems of action and belief that allow people to function and survive. Culture is manifested in our behaviors and beliefs about food, shelter, clothing, space, and time, as well as our value systems. We learn our cultures, and second language learning involves culture learning as well.

Some aspects of culture are not manifested by artifacts or surface behaviors; as a result, they are sometimes difficult to discern. Such "deep" aspects of culture may affect classroom teaching-learning situations.

## ACTIVITIES AND QUESTIONS TO THINK ABOUT

1. Check with your local school district, county office, or state department of education and find out how many language minority children there are in your area. How many of them are limited English proficient? What language groups are represented?
2. BáFá BáFá (Skirts, 1977) is a simulation game designed to develop cross-cultural awareness. The library or instructional resource center on your campus may have the game. Play BáFá BáFá in class and discuss your reactions. Questions provided with the game can guide your discussions.
3. Teachers working with Navajo children need to be careful about field trips to the zoo and to certain museums. Navajo children should not see bears or snakes, nor should they be allowed to view human skeletal remains. If they do so, they must participate in cleansing ceremonies, which are lengthy and often costly. Study an ethnic or cultural group in your area. Use personal resources as well as the library. Are there any areas where you might cause offense without realizing it?
4. An article in a California newspaper ("Cupertino draws Asian immigrants," *San Jose Mercury News,* February 21, 1988, 1A, 6A) indicates that builders are designing homes to meet the demands of Asian buyers. Such houses, for example, should not have stairways that face the front door or face east or west. Think of your own home. Discuss ways in which your house reflects your culture.
5. Early in 1988, Western journalists in China reported with a great deal of excitement that the leading Chinese television newscaster had appeared on the evening news in a Mao suit rather than his usual Western business suit ("In China, wrinkle of change or just a crumpled old suit?" *New York Times,* January 30, 1988, 1, 4). This, they felt, was the harbinger of an important announcement—possibly the death of a high-ranking official or a change of regime. Think of the clothing worn by celebrities and politicians in the United States. What different things can clothing symbolize?
6. Several states permit automobile owners to create their own license plate numbers. In creating the following plates, people have made reference to the kinds of cars they drive:

   • VET4ME
   • MGMS TOY
   • MY RX7

- HOT CAT
- JANS BUG

What kinds of cars do these plates describe? What kinds of linguistic and cultural knowledge do you need to decipher this information?

7. What we say reveals a great deal about our culture. What we don't say is revealing as well. Look at the following list of euphemisms:

- restroom
- powder room
- john
- men's room
- ladies' room
- bathroom

What can you figure out about our culture from this list? What other kinds of things do we generally use euphemisms to describe?

## SUGGESTIONS FOR FURTHER READING

The study of culture includes the study of just about everything. From an academic standpoint, culture is studied by anthropologists, educators, linguists, psychologists, sociologists, and cyberneticists. It is impossible, therefore, to provide a comprehensive list of readings on the subject. In addition to books about the concept of culture in general, an abundance of scholarly literature describes particular cultures as well as cross-cultural communication and conflict.

We cannot, in addition, exclude the realm of fiction. The works of Isaac Bashevis Singer, Maxine Hong Kingston, Ernesto Galarza, Toni Morrison, Amy Tan, and Ntozake Shange are a tiny sampling of the possibilities. Tony Hillerman's popular series of mystery novels set on the Navajo reservation provides fascinating insights into Navajo and Hopi cultures. The list below reviews books that highlight points in this chapter. It may serve as a starting point for additional reading.

Arvizu, S. F., Snyder, W. A., & Espinosa, P. T. (1980).
*Demystifying the concept of culture: Theoretical and conceptual tools.* Los Angeles: Evaluation, Dissemination and Assessment Center, California State University, Los Angeles.
An analysis of the nature of culture, with illustrative examples, this monograph contains clear, useful information for teachers in training.

Hall, E. T. (1959). *The silent language.* Garden City, NY: Doubleday.
Hall defines culture as communication and analyzes modalities of communication—including language, space, and time—from a cross-cultural perspective.

Hall, E. T. (1966). *The hidden dimension.* Garden City, NY: Doubleday.
An examination of people's use of space in public and in private from an anthropological perspective, this classic book contains fascinating explanations and examples of concepts of proxemics.

Spradley, J. P. (Ed.). ( 1972). *Culture and cognition: Rules, maps, and plans.* San Francisco: Chandler.

The central theme of this book is the nature and structure of culture. Articles from the fields of anthropology, economics, linguistics, psychology, and sociology provide a wide variety of perspectives and examples.

Valdes, J. M. (1986). *Culture bound: Bridging the cultural gap in language teaching.* New York: Cambridge University Press.

Part 1 of this book presents a theoretical foundation about the relationship of culture, thought, and language. Part 2 describes cultural traits of several groups to alert language teachers to the characteristics of their students. Articles in Part 3 relate to classroom applications and present practical suggestions for working with non-native speakers of a language.

# chapter 9

# Culture and Academic Success

Analyses of the differences between cultures are often used to attempt to explain differences in educational performance among ethnic groups. Differential achievement has been viewed from a variety of perspectives, which will be discussed in this chapter. Some theorists have proposed that different groups have varying abilities that are genetically determined. Others have suggested that some cultures are inadequate or lacking in basic ingredients that are necessary for children to succeed in school.

A third viewpoint that has gained popularity is the cultural mismatch view. Mismatch theorists suggest that different groups have communication and learning styles that don't fit with mainstream styles usually found in classrooms. The mismatch model does not address the entire problem, but understanding communication and learning styles is essential for teachers. This concept will be treated in some detail in this chapter.

It has been suggested that analysis of differential achievement among groups must go beyond analysis of teacher and student interaction in the classroom and has to be seen in the political and social context of the wider society. We will discuss the contextual interaction model here.

Finally, any analysis of achievement must consider the nature of measurement. Testing is not ideologically innocent; differential outcomes may well be the product of biases in the procedures and content of assessment measures. This chapter will include a discussion of culture bias in standardized testing.

## GENETIC INFERIORITY

The genetic inferiority model assumes that certain groups are inherently incapable of intellectual achievement. Rooted in nineteenth-century colonialism, genetic inferiority was a convenient way of justifying cultural domination and enslavement. In current thinking, it has similar convenience value: it blames the victim and eliminates the need for any transformation of our education systems—if heredity is at fault, there simply are no solutions.

An article by A. R. Jensen published in the *Harvard Educational Review* in 1969 sparked the current debate on the relationship between heredity and academic ability. In that article, Jensen suggested that a person's intellectual ability is determined 80 percent by heredity and 20 percent by environment; hence, most differences in achievement between groups are based in genetic factors. Scholars have criticized Jensen's work extensively (Cortés, 1986; Feuerstein, 1978; Ogbu, 1978), and research generally disproves the notion that intellectual ability is genetically determined and inalterable. However, this unfortunate perspective has remarkable staying power. For example, in a 1988 survey of science teachers, 26 percent of the 200 respondents replied "definitely true" or "probably true" to an item that stated, "Some races of people are more intelligent than others" ("Study reveals . . .," 1988).

More recently, in *The Bell Curve,* Charles Murray and Richard J. Herrnstein (1994) have reasserted the idea that white people are more intelligent than black people as a result of genetic factors. Despite widespread criticism (Beardsley, 1995; "Reacting to *The bell curve,*" 1995; Kamin, 1995) of Murray and Herrnstein's assumptions and methodology, the book has captured the attention of a public frustrated by what they perceive as the inefficacy of government programs and the failure of schooling to address the problem of underachievement among minority groups.

## CULTURAL DEFICIT

The cultural deficit or deficiency model suggests that ethnic minorities fail in school because their cultures are inadequate in some way. The deficit view gained popularity in the 1960s, when it was suggested, for example, that black children suffered from language deprivation as a result of inadequate language development in their home backgrounds (Bereiter & Engelmann, 1966).

As we have seen, all cultures are rich and complex and, like languages, evolve to suit the needs of particular groups. African Americans, like other groups, have a coherent culture. Black American culture in particular includes a vibrant and dynamic tradition of oral language—as witnessed, for example, by the richness of the  African American preaching heritage. The notion that black children are deprived somehow of language experience is clearly a case of cultural tunnel vision.

The cultural deficit view blames the victims but assumes that the deficit is correctable and offers the possibility of solutions through remediation. Critics, however, suggest that remediation efforts have proven ineffective and that, furthermore, the deficit view fails to account for the social and political context of schooling (Boykin, 1984).

## CULTURAL MISMATCH

The cultural mismatch model suggests that members of minority groups do not succeed in school because the characteristics of their cultures are incongruent with those of the mainstream group and the school system. This view is supported by the work of researchers who have analyzed learning styles. Culture traits that are part of learning style and that may affect classroom dynamics include cognitive styles, communicative styles, and interaction styles—features that often overlap.

While differences in learning styles may not be the entire explanation for differential achievement among groups, they warrant a detailed look. Such traits are part of what might be called *invisible* or *deep* culture. Teachers need to understand and acknowledge aspects of culture beyond material manifestations.

### A Note on Methodology

In order to study communication and interaction in classrooms, education has borrowed a study method from anthropology called *ethnography*. An ethnographic study describes a culture. The basic research question for an ethnographer, however, is not, "What do I see these people doing?" but rather "What do these people see themselves doing?" (Spradley & McCurdy, 1972, p. 9). Rather than beginning with categories or models of interaction and then gathering data to support them, ethnographers first gather data and then identify categories that emerge from the information.

An ethnographic study of a classroom assumes that each classroom is a microculture of its own. Ethnographic studies of classrooms often involve extensive tape recordings and videotapes of the proceedings, as well as interviews with the participants, which are then analyzed for patterns of interaction.

### Cognitive Style

Cognitive styles are ways of thinking or problem solving. For example, sometimes we acknowledge that a person is particularly good at understanding "the big picture." On the other hand, we might refer to a friend or a colleague as "detail-oriented." In these examples, we are making reference to a person's cognitive style.

Similarly, it has been proposed that some people are field dependent or field sensitive, whereas others are field independent. Field sensitive students prefer to work cooperatively; field independent students prefer competitive learning situations. Field sensitive students are motivated by their relationship to their teacher; they seek social rewards. Field independent students are task-oriented and motivated by nonsocial rewards.

Ramírez and Castañeda (1974) suggested that Mexican American students, as a result of cultural values and socialization practices, tend to be more field dependent than their Anglo counterparts or than Anglo teachers. Lack of congruence between the cognitive styles of Mexican American children and the expectations of the school environment was offered as an explanation for their failure to achieve in school. The children who succeeded had become bicultural—that is, bicognitive, or able to cope with the differing demands of more than one culture.

The notion of biculturalism as bicognitivism is thought-provoking and controversial. Critics, however, have suggested that the rate and manner of cognitive development are demonstrably the same for Mexican American children and Anglo children. Also, recent demographic analyses of U.S. Hispanics has spotlighted the complexity of Hispanic culture and demonstrated that many previously common assumptions about how Hispanics live were false. Consequently, the cognitive style analysis has been seen as an oversimplification of issues affecting the achievement of Mexican American students.

Subsequent research into patterns of interaction and communication, however, demonstrates that there are discernible differences between parental and community socialized behaviors and expectations that minority children bring to school and the environment they encounter there.

## Communication Style

The common assumption that all parties to a particular interaction are assigning similar meanings to the subject at hand often leads to miscommunication. Awareness of the possible pitfalls in cross-cultural communication has led to books and articles that analyze cultural differences for the benefit of business people involved in international negotiations (Pfeiffer, 1988). Handbooks in the popular press present do's and don'ts for travelers to avoid misunderstandings in foreign countries.

However, subtleties of communication style difference often go unnoticed in classroom situations, and they may cause misunderstandings that affect children's ability to achieve and succeed. One study (Gumperz, 1981) analyzed the difference between black and white children's reactions to a classroom task. African American children appeared slower to settle down, were more likely to ask for help, and said things like "I can't do this" or "I don't know," even after they had received instruction. Researchers noted that their comments repeatedly had an identifiable pattern of intonation.

Black adult judges were asked to analyze tape recordings of the black children's verbal responses. Their understanding of the children's comments was that the children were expressing a desire for company while they worked, rather than an actual inability to do the work itself. Failure on the part of a teacher to understand the intention of the children's remarks might lead to the assumption that the students were incapable of understanding or completing the assigned task, which was not the case.

## Interaction Style

Patterns of classroom interaction determine who participates, how they participate, and when. For example, a teacher can interact with all students as a group. In that format, a teacher can either address all the students or address individuals while the rest look on. Students may be asked to respond as a group or individually. Sometimes students respond voluntarily; other times they are called on. In these situations, the teacher generally structures the interaction.

In other patterns, the class may be divided into small groups, with one group interacting with the teacher while others work independently. In some cases, all the students in a class may work independently, with the teacher functioning as a monitor or resource. Students may also work in small groups, with selected individuals taking leadership roles. Variations of this format are gaining popularity as cooperative-learning-based curricula are developed. (See Chapter 6 for a discussion of cooperative learning.)

The way in which interaction is structured has an impact on student participation. It has been noted, for example, that Native American children seem to be unable or unwilling to participate verbally in classroom interactions. Analyses of classroom interaction styles indicate that patterns of classroom interaction are often incongruent with traditional Native American interaction patterns.

Susan Philips (1983) studied the interaction styles of school children from the Warm Springs Indian Reservation in Oregon. Examining communication patterns among adult members of the community to determine their interaction styles, she found that Warm Springs Indian children's patterns of discourse and interaction differ from the usual communication patterns found in their classrooms. The children have been socialized to interact in patterns appropriate for their community.

According to Philips, "Indian organization of interaction can be characterized as maximizing the control that an individual has over his or her own turn at talk, and as minimizing the control that a given individual has over the turns of others" (p. 115). Consequently, Indian children were much less likely than non-Indian children to respond in situations where they were called upon involuntarily, or where they were singled out. On the other hand, the Indian children in the study participated verbally in small-group situations where students were allowed to control their own interactions.

In another study of American Indian classrooms (Mohatt & Erickson, 1981) researchers analyzed the differences between an Indian and a non-Indian teacher in an Odawa school in Canada. The researchers noted differences in pacing, the directiveness of the teachers, and the structures used to stimulate participation. The Indian teacher's classroom was organized at a slower pace and seemed to be more responsive to the students' readiness to move to a particular activity. The Indian teacher paused longer to wait for responses and engaged in more face-to-face private interactions than the non-Indian teacher. The Indian teacher used small-group work to a far greater extent than the non-Indian counterpart.

Interaction during reading instruction was analyzed in the Kamehameha Early Education Program (KEEP) in Honolulu (Au & Jordan, 1981). As a result of that research, KEEP has successfully developed reading skills with Hawaiian children by structuring lessons to make them similar to Hawaiian talk stories, a traditional form of didactic storytelling.

Studies of interaction style are of particular interest. In many cases, the children involved are English speaking or even English monolingual but still experience difficulties in classroom settings that are culturally inappropriate to their experience. This leads us to the conclusion that we must consider factors beyond language in dual language instructional settings.

## Cultural Mismatch: Does It Answer the Question?

The cultural mismatch perspective does not assign responsibility for school failure to anyone in particular. It does suggest that members of ethnic groups need to acculturate and become more "Americanized," while, at the same time, schools need to recognize and accommodate children's cultural differences.

Cultural mismatch is an attractive perspective in that it offers tangible solutions. Critics, however, suggest that this view is oversimplified. If differential achievement is a matter of miscommunication, why don't students and teachers negotiate solutions among themselves? People generally overcome obstacles to communication, even in complex situations, altering their communicative style and sometimes developing whole new languages to interact with others (McDermott & Gospodinoff, 1981).

Is it possible that minority children in school fail to negotiate miscommunications because they resist the notion of acculturation? Acculturation, after all, implies the superiority of a particular group (Sue & Padilla, 1986). Overall, the cultural mismatch view, while revealing in individual classroom situations, fails to take into account the larger social and political context of education (Cummins, 1984a).

## CONTEXTUAL INTERACTION

Cross-cultural miscommunication has attracted interest, for example, in the area of business, where it has been noted that failure on the part of North Americans to understand differences in communication styles has been embarrassing and costly. In the area of education, dual language classrooms eliminate obvious language barriers to understanding and accomplishment. And, as discussed above, microstudies of classroom interactions allow us to develop strategies to maximize opportunities for culturally diverse students to participate and succeed.

But interaction patterns within individual classrooms account only for the teacher-child relationship, which is but one small segment of the entire network of relationships that affect children in school. Critics of the cultural mismatch theory suggest that the mismatch view is too narrow and that it fails to explain why some groups of language minority children do well in school despite cultural difference and language barriers (Ogbu & Matute-Bianchi, 1986).

Koreans are a case in point. Korean students, descendants of forced laborers brought to Japan in the 1930s, do not do well in Japanese schools, where they are a minority. In the United States, on the other hand, Korean students, like many other Asians, have a tendency to excel. This example is not unique— comparable patterns arise in many places around the world. Why, then, do some minorities do poorly in some settings and well in others?

The contextual interaction model recognizes that there are differences between ethnic minority cultures and mainstream values that may be prevalent in schools. Unlike the mismatch model, however, contextual interaction suggests that there is a dynamic power relationship between minority cultures and schooling which must be analyzed from a broad social and political perspective (Cortés, 1986).

## JOHN OGBU'S TYPOLOGY

Some minorities do well in school; others do not. Some reasons for this inconsistency become apparent if we recognize that not all minorities have the same political and social status. John Ogbu (1978) has categorized minorities into three distinct groups. Success in school, according to Ogbu, is different for members of each of these groups, in keeping with the characteristics he has described.

### Autonomous Minorities

Jews and Mormons are examples of autonomous minorities in the United States. While they are definitely minorities in the numerical sense, they are not perceived as second-class citizens. They maintain a distinct cultural identity but are not socially or politically isolated.

### Immigrant Minorities

Immigrants have moved to the United States for a variety of reasons, but to some extent it is possible to say that they have come here voluntarily. While they may be socially and politically subordinated and economically disadvantaged, they maintain a positive self-concept.

Some immigrants have come from societies where they were socialized as majority group members and have internalized a sense of their own power. They perceive the disadvantages in their new setting as temporary and alterable. Cubans who took refuge in the United States after the Cuban revolution, for example, were often highly educated professionals and business people who quickly entered the U.S. mainstream.

Many immigrants feel that despite the inconveniences of their new circumstances, their situation has improved in the United States. A woman living in a two-room shack with four children told me that her life is better in the United States than in her country of origin because "back home with all of us working we ate meat once a week. Here we can eat meat every day."

Suarez-Orozco and Suarez-Orozco (1993) used the Thematic Apperception Test to study the attitudes of immigrant high school students from Central America. They concluded that the students they worked with were motivated to work hard in school as a compensation for feelings of guilt, resulting from having left families behind, often to endure hardships so that they themselves might have better opportunities.

## Castelike Minorities

Sometimes called *indigenous* or *traditional minorities,* castelike minorities "have become incorporated into a society more or less involuntarily and permanently through slavery, conquest, or colonization and then relegated to menial status" (Ogbu & Matute-Bianchi, 1986, p. 90). Castelike or indigenous minorities in the United States include African Americans, who were brought here as slaves, and Native Americans, who were subordinated by conquest. Mexican Americans were originally a conquered people, and newly arrived Mexican immigrants acquire subordinate status as they enter the preexisting infrastructure that makes Mexican Americans a castelike minority.

## Secondary Cultural Differences

Ogbu (1994) points out that attempts to rectify inequality between minority and dominant culture groups are most often implemented at the instrumental level (i.e., by attempting to provide equal access to educational and material resources). Such attempts, ineffective in and of themselves, also ignore relational differences between groups.

For example, minority groups develop a set of cultural characteristics that arise in contact with the dominant culture, which allow minority group members to function in social settings where they are subordinated (Ogbu, 1992).

In Ogbu's view, members of caste-like groups may in fact engage in what he calls "cultural inversion," or ". . . the tendency . . . to regard certain forms of behavior, events, symbols, and meanings as inappropriate . . . because these are characteristic of White Americans" (Ogbu, 1992, p. 8). Among some black students, for example, succeeding in school is equated with "acting white" (Fordham, 1991). Similarly, young women may avoid success in school because academic success contradicts the images they have internalized as feminine (Bell, 1991). In other words, being too successful might equate with "acting male."

Foley (1994) notes that Ogbu's theory of oppositional culture is a negative characterization that fails to acknowledge the "positive, self-valorizing character of oppositional ethnic humor, dialect, musical, and street art forms" (p. 187).

Referring to his own research in a South Texas high school, Foley notes that despite the historical and social context in that region, many Mexican American students have achieved success without relinquishing a sense of their own ethnicity. At least in the particular situation Foley studied, students whom Ogbu might characterize as involuntary or castelike minorities appeared to function in a manner more congruent with voluntary minorities. Foley encourages us to focus our research on why some involuntary minority students succeed rather than why some fail.

## STATUS, POWER, AND SCHOOL SUCCESS

People sometimes fail to realize the nature and amount of power that schools represent. Schooling in the United States is compulsory—all children must attend. For members of the economic and social mainstream, taking their children to the schoolhouse door is often emotional but not necessarily intimidating or threatening. For people whose cultural, social, economic, or political perspectives differ from the mainstream, schools may represent a power structure that will indoctrinate their children away from the ways of living that their families value and cherish.

Choice in schooling is generally reserved for the more affluent members of our society, and awareness of options in schooling is most often the privilege of the educated. Most children attend the neighborhood public school; there is relatively little choice in the matter. Schools, therefore, become what Henry Giroux (1988) has called "contested sites," arenas for political power struggles.

Such struggles take a number of forms. The debate, for example, regarding evolution versus creationism is a curriculum battle that has been waged furiously for over 50 years and continues unabated today. Other areas of tension are manifested in censorship battles, where texts or materials in the school library may be at issue; and home schooling conflicts, where parents or a group of parents may resist the notion of a majority-imposed curriculum (Arons, 1983).

Preservice teachers often comment with surprise on the disparity between the behavior of minority children at home, where they are required to carry out important responsibilities, such as providing income and caring for younger siblings or elderly grandparents, and the behavior of the same children in school, where they may be irresponsible and even disruptive. The behavior of those children makes it clear that they do not respect or feel respected in the school environment.

## The Role of Schools as Perceived by Minority Students

Members of autonomous and immigrant minority groups are more likely to succeed in school than members of castelike minority groups. Children are astute sociologists, quickly making accurate sense of the world around them. Children

who are members of castelike minorities perceive that society has placed limitations on their aspirations and that schools serve as instruments for preserving
the power status quo.

Ogbu and Matute-Bianchi (1986) suggest that the role of schools becomes
part of folk culture, handed down from one generation to the next. Among
castelike minority groups, school is not seen as a way of getting ahead. The
motion picture *Stand and Deliver* (Menendez, Musca, & Olmos, 1988) tells the
true story of Jaime Escalante, a Bolivian-born schoolteacher, and his first year
in an urban high school in Los Angeles. Escalante's entire math class, with many
students who could not manage basic mathematics at the outset, passed the
Advanced Placement calculus test.

In one striking scene, a student asks Escalante for an extra book to keep at
home so his friends won't see him looking studious. He is not yet ready to give
up his identity in a social setting that assures him success, to take on the identity of a student, in a world he mistrusts and may not be able to master.

The students who did pass the Advanced Placement test were accused of
cheating and were required to take the test again. The students were subse-
quently vindicated, but the accusation corroborates the contextual interaction
model and speaks to the accurate awareness minority students may have that
they are not welcomed by the system.

## Contextual Interaction as a Solution to Differential Achievement

Contextual interaction, unlike the genetic inferiority or cultural deficit views,
does not blame the victim. And while it incorporates the notion of cultural
mismatch as part of the explanation for differential achievement, it suggests that
we have to seek solutions beyond the classroom door. Contextual interaction
requires that we consider the complex network of factors that schooling involves.
Issues of social, cultural, political, and economic empowerment must be considered if we are to ascertain why some children fail where others succeed.

## TESTING AND CULTURAL DIVERSITY

When we posit that cultural minorities do not achieve in school, the question
must arise, "What is achievement, and how do we define and measure it?" A
discussion of achievement must therefore include a discussion of measurement.
Literally millions of standardized tests are administered annually that purport to
measure academic activity, emotional and social characteristics, and vocational
talent. These tests are gatekeepers for many important opportunities and are
often constructed around standards of normalcy that are not reflective of or
appropriate for groups whose members are not white or socially and economically middle class.

## Discriminatory Testing

The issue of discriminatory testing has come to the fore in the field of special education. Minority students historically have been overrepresented in special-education settings. The landmark federal court decision in *Diana v. State Board of Education* in California in 1970 established the right of minority students to nonbiased assessments. The Education for All Handicapped Children Act of 1975 (P.L. 94-142) is a federal law that seeks to ensure due-process rights for exceptional children and their parents and spotlights the need for nondiscriminatory assessment procedures. In view of such legislation and litigation, educators, psychologists, and psychometrists have begun to consider the bias in testing in several areas.

***Content and Construct Bias.***   Bias may exist in the language used in a test. For example, as we saw in Chapter 3, vocabulary may differ among regions or social classes. A monkey is a *mono* to a Puerto Rican Spanish-speaking child and a *chango* in the southwestern United States. Test items that use standard language forms may be perplexing to children who speak regional or social variants of a language.

In addition, most standardized tests are constructed around the values and experiences of mainstream middle-class culture, which minority children may not know or understand. A study of testing in Costa Rica highlights what happens when standardized tests are given to children from a different culture (Howard, 1982). Costa Rican children did poorly compared to their U.S. counterparts on tests of short-term memory involving the repetition of series of numbers. Middle-class children in the United States are exposed to number series quite young because of the emphasis placed on knowing addresses and phone numbers. On the other hand, noting that Costa Rican children scored higher than U.S. counterparts on tests of visual memory, Howard conjectured that it might be the result of orienting in an environment where landmarks and descriptions are more important than addresses.

Examples of content bias closer to home are common and may crop up unexpectedly. I observed a white middle-class child during a kindergarten readiness assessment. The examiner asked him to identify an object in a black-and-white line drawing that looked something like the drawing in Figure 9.1. The child pondered for a moment and identified the object as a plate. The examiner was surprised that the child failed to recognize a telephone dial. On further questioning, it became clear that the child was well versed in the ways of the

**FIGURE 9.1**   Drawing shown in kindergarten readiness test

telephone—up to and including computerized preprogrammed dialing—but had never seen or used anything but a pushbutton phone!

To some extent, from a minority perspective, standardized tests measure a child's degree of assimilation or "Americanization." Puerto Rican children, for example, when asked to complete the phrase "bread and _____" will often respond with "bread and coffee." The combination of bread and coffee is as linguistically and semantically logical to a Puerto Rican child as the combination of ham and eggs might be to a mainstream middle-class child, and every bit as appropriate for breakfast.

*Standardization.*    Prior to the 1970s, when litigation and legislation prodded educators to action, it was common for standardization samples to be all white. Inclusion of limited numbers of nonwhite children in standardization samples still does not respond adequately to the changing demographics of American society, where "minorities" are rapidly becoming the majority population in many areas.

*Testers, Test Takers, and Test Situations.*    Personnel who administer tests in school are often monolingual and members of the majority culture. They may have unconscious biases toward minority children. In an attempt to make tests fair, teachers or psychologists sometimes administer them using interpreters. Often interpreters are teachers' aides who may not be fully proficient in both languages or trained in test procedures.

Children from minority backgrounds may be intimidated by the test administrator or the test situation. Also, tests may require children to produce elaborate verbal responses. Children from many cultures may respond only briefly to questions as a sign of respect for an adult or authority figure.

Many tests are carefully timed. In cases where test takers are working in their second language, time constraints present a disadvantage. In addition, a child whose culture does not have a Euro-Western orientation to time may not respond the same way to timed tests as middle-class white children.

## Nondiscriminatory Testing

Having recognized biases in testing, educators have tried several approaches to correct them.

*Translation.*    Test translation is attractive, since it appears simple and inexpensive and does not require the development of new tests. There are, however, significant disadvantages to translated tests. Translations do not eliminate and may even aggravate content bias. Consider, for example, the word *bat*, a one-syllable English word, easily decoded by a beginning reader. The word *bat* translates in Spanish to *murciélago,* a polysyllabic word with an irregular accent, far beyond the skills of an early reader. Such examples are numerous; they serve to illustrate the difficulties inherent in translating tests.

***Establishing Differential Norms.***    The establishing of differential norms involves minimal or no alteration in a particular test but creates different standards for different ethnic groups. This is particularly unsatisfactory as a solution because it reinforces stereotyping, building in negative expectations of a particular group that may actually cause negative results.

***Culture-Fair Tests.***    Sometimes called *culture-specific tests,* culture-fair tests are designed to assess abilities with reference to the specific values and expectations of a child's own culture or subculture. Even if it were possible to construct a test to respond to the complexities of every subculture, these tests would still have questionable value. For one thing, culture-fair tests would provide little information about a child's ability to function in a mainstream setting. Also, while culture-fair testing addresses the issue of content bias, it does not solve the problem of test procedures and their impact on children of diverse backgrounds.

***Culture-Free Tests.***    Culture-free tests attempt to assess those areas of functioning that are assumed to be cross-cultural—that is, equally common to people in most cultures. One critic has offered a particularly succinct criticism of culture-free tests: "A culture-free test would presumably probe learnings which have not been affected by environment; this is sheer nonsense" (Wesman, 1969, p. 269).

***Comprehensive Testing.***    It may be possible to resolve the problems presented by standardized testing for minority children by broadening the scope of the testing itself or by lessening the impact of testing by considering additional information from parents and teachers.

One model devised for assessing children from culturally diverse backgrounds is the System of Multicultural Pluralistic Assessment, or SOMPA (Mercer & Lewis, 1979). SOMPA uses a comprehensive array of tests to try to create a complete picture of a child's abilities in a way that is sensitive to the child's experiences and values. The test includes a medical component, which looks for health-related or physical factors that might interfere with learning; a component for assessing social skills, which includes an inventory completed by the child's parents; and a pluralistic component, which estimates the child's learning potential in comparison to children from similar backgrounds.

## Learning Potential

The work of Reuven Feuerstein (1978) has important implications for the instruction of minority children who do not succeed in school. Feuerstein asks us to redefine the term *culturally deprived.* In his approach, *culturally deprived* does not refer to the idea that a person belongs to a culture which is inadequate in some way.

In Feuerstein's framework, the term applies instead to a person who has not been the recipient of culturally transmitted information. A culturally deprived person is one for whom the world has not been mediated, explained, or handed down in a meaningful fashion. Cultural deprivation of this kind may occur with children from any background. A social service professional, commenting in the *New York Times* on the causes of violence among young people, remarked that many children "have no memories, no rituals and no traditions." She reports that she asked one teenager to tell her something the child's family did every year, and the child could not respond. She goes on to observe, "That may not sound like a big deal, but memories of a daddy building a snow fort become a road map for the future" (Butterfield, 1994, p. A11). Minority children may lack cultural transmission as a result of social and political circumstances.

It has been suggested that the expression *culturally deprived* is powerfully linked to the concept of a deficient culture. To use those words to describe a substantially different concept may be confusing and potentially dangerous (Cummins, 1984a). Terminology aside, the concept is a useful and significant one.

Feuerstein suggests that the lack of mediating experiences is highly correctable through appropriate training, once areas of difficulty have been assessed. His proposed form of assessment, the Learning Potential Assessment Device, measures the ability of a child to perform before and after instruction in a particular task. This model has potential for assessing a child's abilities without the pitfalls of bias often found in other kinds of testing.

## SUMMARY

Educators have devised several theoretical frameworks to explain differential achievement among diverse ethnic groups. The genetic inferiority model suggests that ability is innate and consequently inalterable. The cultural deficit model posits that some cultures are inadequate.

The cultural mismatch model proposes that children come to school with values and behaviors that don't fit the school environment. Cultural mismatch theorists have provided some significant insights into culture differences in communication, but the model does not account for the fact that some children succeed in spite of language and culture difference. The contextual interaction model suggests that the failure of some children to achieve in school can be explained only by taking political and social factors into account.

Achievement in school is measured, and emphasis is often placed on the results of standardized tests. Such tests are often biased against children from minority cultures. Biases appear in content, norming, and testing procedures. Various attempts to correct biases in testing include: translation, ethnic norms, culture-fair tests, culture-free tests, comprehensive testing, and assessment of learning potential.

## ACTIVITIES AND QUESTIONS TO THINK ABOUT

1. Look up demographics for your local school district(s). School district offices may have this information. Local newspapers sometimes report on demographic changes. How has the population changed in the last 10 years?

2. Look up recent citations under *academic achievement* and *minority achievement* in the publications prepared under the U.S. Office of Education by the Educational Resources Information Center (ERIC). Survey titles and abstracts to see which approach researchers are using to analyze minority student achievement.

3. The letter below describes the way a Native American child would have been raised. How is this child's socialization different from that of a mainstream white middle-class child? What problems might a Native American child encounter in a typical public school classroom? What can you do in your classroom to meet the needs of children from diverse cultural backgrounds?

*Dear Teacher:*

*Before you take charge of the classroom that contains my child, please ask yourself why you are going to teach Indian children. What are your expectations? What rewards do you anticipate? What ego-needs will our children have to meet?*

*Write down and examine all the information and opinions you possess about Indians. What are the stereotypes and untested assumptions that you bring with you into the classroom? How many negative attitudes towards Indians will you put before my child?*

*What values, class prejudices and moral principles do you take for granted as universal? Please remember that "different from" is not the same as "worse than" or "better than," and the yardstick you use to measure your own life satisfactorily may not be appropriate for their lives.*

*The term culturally deprived was invented by well-meaning middle-class whites to describe something they could not understand.*

*Too many teachers, unfortunately, seem to see their role as rescuer. My child does not need to be rescued; he does not consider being Indian a misfortune. He has a culture, probably older than yours; he has meaningful values and a rich and varied experiential background. However strange or incomprehensible it may seem to you, you have no right to do or say anything that implies to him that it is less than satisfactory.*

*Our children's experiences have been different from those of the "typical" white middle-class child for whom most school curricula seem to have been designed. (I suspect that this "typical" child does not exist except in the minds of curriculum writers.) Nonetheless, my child's experiences have been as intense and meaningful to him as any child's.*

*Like most Indian children his age, he is competent. He can dress himself, prepare a meal for himself, clean up afterwards, care for a younger child. He knows his Reserve, all of which is his home, like the back of his hand.*

*He is not accustomed to having to ask permission to do the ordinary things that are part of normal living. He is seldom forbidden to do anything; more usually the consequences of an action are explained to him and he is allowed to decide for himself whether or not to act. His entire existence since he has been old enough to see and hear has been an experiential learning situation, arranged to provide him with the opportunity to develop his skills and confidence in his own capacities. Didactic teaching will be an alien experience for him.*

*He is not self-conscious in the way many white children are. Nobody has ever told him his efforts towards independence are cute. He is a young human being energetically doing his job, which is to get on with the process of learning to function as an adult human being. He will respect you as a person, but he will expect you to do likewise to him.*

*He has been taught, by precept, that courtesy is an essential part of human conduct and rudeness is any action that makes another person feel stupid or foolish. Do not mistake his patient courtesy for indifference or passivity.*

*He doesn't speak standard English, but he is no way "linguistically handicapped." If you will take the time and courtesy to listen and observe carefully, you will see that he and the other Indian children communicate very well, both among themselves and with other Indians. They speak "functional English," very effectively augmented by their fluency in the silent language, the subtle, unspoken communication of facial expressions, gestures, body movement and the use of personal space.*

*You will be well advised to remember that our children are skillful interpreters of the silent language. They will know your feelings and attitudes with unerring precision, no matter how carefully you arrange your smile or modulate your voice. They will learn in your classroom, because children learn involuntarily. What they learn will depend on you.*

*Will you help my child to learn to read, or will you teach him that he has a reading problem? Will you help him develop problem-solving skills, or will you teach him that school is where you try to guess what answer the teacher wants?*

*Will he learn that his sense of his own value and dignity is valid, or will he learn that he must forever be apologetic and "trying harder" because he isn't white? Can you help him acquire the intellectual skills he needs without at the same time imposing your values on top of those he already has?*

*Respect my child. He is a person. He has a right to be himself.*
*Yours very sincerely,*
*His Mother*

4. Analyze your community in terms of Ogbu's categories. Who are representatives of each?

5. How is academic achievement reported in your state/district? What tests are used? How are scores grouped? What patterns can you discern? Testing information may be available from your state department of education or from local district offices. Test results are sometimes reported in local newspapers.

6. Investigate placement procedures for special education in your local district. How is cultural diversity accommodated in the process?

---

* **Source**: "Respect My Child: He Has a Right to Be Himself." Wassaja, February, 1976. Reprinted by permission of *The Indian Historian*.

# SUGGESTIONS FOR FURTHER READING

California State Department of Education (Ed.). (1986). *Beyond language: Social and cultural factors in schooling language minority students.* Los Angeles: Evaluation, Dissemination, and Assessment Center, California State University, Los Angeles.
This book was constructed as a companion piece for *Schooling and Language Minority Students: A Theoretical Framework* (now in its second edition) and *Studies on Immersion Education: A Collection for United States Educators,* edited by the California State Department of Education (see Chapters 1 and 6). The *Framework* and *Immersion* address educational issues of first and second language. *Beyond Language* considers social and cultural factors that have an impact on the education of language minority students.
  Providing theoretical analyses and data that support the contextual interaction model, *Beyond Language* is basic reading for those concerned with the relationship of sociocultural factors and schooling.

Cummins, J. (1984a). *Bilingualism and special education: Issues in assessment and pedagogy.* San Diego: College-Hill Press.
An analysis of the basic assumptions underlying assessment of achievement, this book discusses bias in testing and considers the effects of bilingualism and culture difference on the school performance of minority children.

Igoa, C. (1995). *The inner world of the immigrant child.* New York: St. Martin's Press.
This is a first-person account of the author's experiences as a teacher of immigrant children and an immigrant herself. Through her story and the stories of her children, she describes how she developed her philosophy and her methodology. Each chapter ends with a summary that provides concrete suggestions for teachers working with immigrant students.

Langer, J. A. (Ed.). (1987). *Language, literacy, and culture: Issues of society and schooling.* Norwood, NJ: Ablex.
A collection of articles from several disciplines, this book analyzes the relationship between language and literacy, learning, and sociocultural factors.

Ogbu, J. U. (1978). *Minority education and caste: The American system in cross-cultural perspective.* New York: Academic Press.
Ogbu presents a structural argument for the underachievement of minority children in school. The contextual interaction model owes much to his analysis of schooling for minority children in cross-cultural settings. Articles by this author are included in *Beyond Language* and *Language, Literacy, and Culture.*

Philips, S. U. (1983). *The invisible culture: Communication in the classroom and the community on the Warm Springs Indian Reservation.* White Plains, NY: Longman.
In this fascinating work, the author studies communication patterns among adults in the Warm Springs Indian community and then analyzes the mismatch between the expectations Warm Springs Indian children have in communication settings and what they encounter in classrooms.

Samuda, R. J., & Woods, S. L. (Eds.). (1983). *Perspectives in immigrant and minority education.* Lanham, MD: University Press of America.
A collection of papers presented at a seminar and a conference held in 1981 at Florida International University, this volume presents discussions of the philosophy of multicultural education, studies of ethnicity and immigration among several communities, and strategies for assessment and development of curricula for diverse students.

Saravia-Shore, M., & Arvizu, S. F. (1992). *Cross-cultural literacy: Ethnographies of communication in multiethnic classrooms.* New York: Garland.

This is a collection of studies which use microethnography to analyze multiethnic classrooms as well as schools in the context of their communities. The introduction provides an excellent overview of anthropological approaches to studying education. Articles included cover a broad scope of community and school settings as well as ethnicities.

Trueba, H. T. (Ed.). (1987). *Success or failure? Learning and the language minority student.* Rowley, MA: Newbury House.

Authors of the articles in this volume consider schooling for language minority students at both the broad sociological level and the immediate classroom interactional level.

Trueba, H. T., Guthrie, G. P., & Au, K. H. (Eds.). (1981). *Culture and the bilingual classroom: Studies in classroom ethnography.* Rowley, MA: Newbury House.

The studies in this volume use microethnography to focus on patterns of interaction between teachers and ethnically diverse students in schools and classrooms. Included are a study of teaching styles in an Odawa school (Gerald Mohatt and Frederick Erickson) and a discussion of the KEEP reading program for Hawaiian students (Kathryn Hu-Pei Au and Cathie Jordan), both of which are often mentioned in analyses of teaching and interaction styles in cross-cultural settings. A section on theoretical and methodological issues is useful to the beginning student of ethnography.

# chapter 10

# Legal Foundations of Dual Language Instruction

$\mathbf{A}$s we saw earlier, dual language instruction was widely available in the United States in the nineteenth century but became unpopular in reaction to large-scale European immigration. Anti-German feeling was particularly powerful, peaking with the advent of World War I. Because of the strong anti-foreign feelings the war engendered, there was little support for instruction in languages other than English in the period between World War I and World War II.

World War II marked the beginning of the American civil rights movement, initially among African Americans. The civil rights movement came to have significant impacts on education in general and bilingual education in particular. This chapter will review the events that laid the groundwork for the legal foundations of dual language instruction.

The educational rights of limited English proficient children are protected by law in the form of legislation, court decisions, and administrative implementation and enforcement regulations. There is no single piece of legislation or court decision that requires dual language instruction for all limited English proficient children. Instead, there is a complex mesh of statutes and case law that defines the educational entitlements of limited English proficient students and affects the ways programs are funded for them. This chapter will review federal and state legislation and case law regarding dual language instruction and describe their impact on policy and program implementation.

## THE HISTORICAL CONTEXT FOR DUAL LANGUAGE INSTRUCTION: WORLD WAR II AND BEYOND

### World War II and Foreign Language Instruction

Fueled by reactions to large waves of immigration and the imminence of World War I, the popularity of dual language instruction in the nineteenth century dwindled rapidly as anti-foreign and anti-German sentiments reached a fever pitch. Nor did the Armistice end the disfavor into which dual language instruction had fallen. Following World War I, dual language instruction in general fell into disfavor, and even traditional foreign language instruction was viewed with distaste. The state of Nebraska went so far as to outlaw the teaching of foreign languages altogether, but that effort was deterred by a United States Supreme Court decision (*Meyer v. Nebraska,* 1923) that held the prohibition unconstitutional, making a case that is based on the Fourteenth Amendment.

The court case did little to inspire an increase in dual language and foreign language instruction, which remained in public disfavor and suffered from disinterest until World War II. With the onset of that war, a renewed interest in foreign language instruction was triggered by the immediate need for expertise in a variety of languages in order to communicate with our allies and maintain effective intelligence efforts.

The value of bilingualism to the war effort was demonstrated dramatically when the U.S. Marine Corps began using the Navajo language for radio communications. After the Japanese had deciphered all military codes, 400 Navajo marines volunteered to transmit top secret information in their first language, which, ironically, they had been forbidden to speak in many places at home. The Japanese were never able to break the "code," and the Navajo effort made a significant contribution to American military success in the Pacific. Many American lives were saved as a result of the contributions of the Navajo "code talkers."

U.S. servicemen who were fluent in German, Italian, and Japanese were considered extremely valuable. To increase the number of military personnel who could be useful for intelligence gathering, the U.S. Army took a leadership role in developing methodologies for fast and effective foreign language instruction, as discussed in Chapter 7. After World War II, the federal government passed the National Defense Education Act (1958), which included support for foreign language instruction. The experiences of World War II taught the United States that the nation needed expertise in foreign languages as part of our national defense.

### World War II and Civil Rights

In addition to an awareness of the need for expertise in foreign languages, World War II affected many Americans' consciousness about their own status and rights. For indigenous minorities, as well as the children of immigrants, serving in World War II bolstered a self-concept of "Americanness." Having proved their commitment to the United States by offering their lives for their country, members of minorities were no longer willing to be regarded as outsiders or second-class citizens.

For many, military service provided the first opportunity to travel outside the United States (or even outside their home towns) and to experience cultures and life-styles different from their own. Many Americans returned from Europe and Asia, where cultural diversity and multilingualism were the norm, with a more sophisticated view of themselves and American society.

The awareness gained through exposure to different cultures and viewpoints extended beyond acceptance of cultural and linguistic diversity. American military personnel were viewed as liberators, and their presence was greeted with great excitement and gratitude. People literally crawled out of concentration camps in Europe to kiss the feet of American G.I.s. It mattered not at all to the Nazis' victims whether the feet and the people they belonged to were black or white or brown.

It is difficult to imagine how American war veterans felt, having served their country and been hailed as liberators, only to suffer the indignities of legalized segregation and discrimination upon returning home. In 1948, when local authorities in Three Rivers, Texas, refused to bury a Chicano war hero in the local veterans' cemetery, World War II veterans in Corpus Christi, Texas founded the American G.I. Forum. The American G.I. Forum became an organization devoted to fighting discrimination in all areas. The incident in Texas was not the first or only demonstration of racism in our history, and the American G.I. Forum is not the first or only organization devoted to antidiscrimination, but the event shows how World War II had raised the consciousness of minority groups in the United States.

## Brown v. the Board of Education (1954)

This changing American consciousness provided the backdrop for the civil rights movement, which reached its most important legal expression in the U.S. Supreme Court decision in *Brown v. the Board of Education* of Topeka in 1954. The *Brown* decision established the principle that separate facilities that were the product of intentional segregation were inherently unequal, reversing a decision by the Court 58 years earlier that separate but equal facilities, or segregation, constituted equality (*Plessy v. Ferguson,* 1896).

The *Brown* decision was a landmark in U.S. history and had a significant impact on all forms of segregation. For example, it was used to break down segregation on buses, trains, restaurants, and (eventually) housing. But the immediate concern of *Brown* was schooling, and to this day schooling remains an arena in which the impact of *Brown* is continually felt.

Judicial efforts to desegregate the schools have been slowed and often stalled due to the resistance of state and local governments. De facto segregation continues to plague public schools today. Efforts to speed school desegregation included the Civil Rights Act of 1964, which contained provisions strengthening the federal government's ability to enforce desegregation and integration. Title VI of the Civil Rights Act plays a key role in the establishment of the rights of language minority children, as we will discuss later in this chapter.

## The Civil Rights Movement and Dual Language Instruction

Overall, the climate of the times in the late 1950s and early 1960s favored the establishment of dual language programs. As described in Chapter 1, the influx of Cuban refugees and the establishment of bilingual programs for Spanish-speaking children in Florida catalyzed the demand for programs for other non-English-speaking children. The success of the program in Florida, combined with increased ethnic self-awareness among minority groups and the philosophical impetus of the civil rights movement, led to legislation and litigation that established the educational rights of language minority children.

## WHO GOVERNS EDUCATION?

The rights of language minority children are protected by legislation, case law, and other governmental actions. Because much of what we shall discuss is rooted in federal law, it is important to understand the avenues by which the federal government acquires jurisdiction over schooling.

The U.S. Constitution gives the federal government, among other things, the power to coin money, to declare war, and to regulate patents and copyrights and prohibits individual states from acting in those areas without the consent of Congress. The functions not allotted to Congress or prohibited to the states are reserved to the states.

Under this constitutional arrangement, education, which is neither specifically assigned to the federal government nor prohibited to the states, is a state government function. The result is variety in education systems across the states.

For example, organization of school governance varies. Hawaii has one school district; California has over a thousand, some consisting of only one school and some consisting of many. Curriculum and funding mechanisms differ from state to state. If you are a certified teacher who has moved from one state to another, you have encountered the lack of uniformity in educational systems and have discovered that each state has its own certification requirements.

## Federal Involvement in Education

Despite the fact that education is theoretically reserved to the states, the federal government exerts powerful influence on schooling through funding, legislation, and judicial action. The federal government apportions funds for education at all levels and supports services that could not be sustained by state budgets. In 1994, the U.S. Department of Education spent approximately $10 billion dollars on student loans, supplemental and compensatory programs, research, information dissemination, and teacher training. In addition, federal agencies such as the National Science Foundation, the Department of Agriculture, the U.S. Information Agency, and others spent substantial sums for educational programs. Federal spending is accompanied by federal regulation. Federal dollars imply federal influence in the area of education.

The influence of federal spending on education is doubly felt because Title VI of the Civil Rights Act of 1964 requires that institutions which receive federal assistance must not discriminate on the basis of race, color, or national origin. Any institution failing to comply with the Civil Rights Act may lose all its federal funding. Most institutions receive federal funding and must therefore support the government's agenda of protecting minorities.

As we have already seen, the federal government also influences education through judicial action. It might be said, in fact, that the U.S. Supreme Court is the government's most powerful educational decision maker. Almost every analysis of law or policy in education must include consideration of the high court's decisions, which have had a strong impact on areas such as desegregation, religion in schools, student discipline, rights of handicapped and gifted students, and private schooling, to name just a few.

We have considered the impact of the federal government on education in some detail because it has bearing on the education of limited English proficient students through all three areas of influence. Funding, Title VI of the Civil Rights Act, and the U.S. Supreme Court, along with other federal legislation, case law, and regulation, provide a firm foundation for the rights of students who don't speak English.

## THE BILINGUAL EDUCATION ACT (TITLE VII)

In 1968 Congress passed Title VII of the Elementary and Secondary Education Act, or the Bilingual Education Act, and in 1969 appropriated $7.5 million dollars to support its programs. Title VII was directed at children from environments where the dominant language was not English and at those whose families had incomes of less than $3,000 per year. Seventy-six projects were funded during the first year of appropriations, serving 27,000 children (Castellanos, 1983).

The 1974 reauthorization of the act broadened the definition of the children served to include those of limited English-speaking ability and eliminated the income requirements. In 1978 the population to be served was again redefined to include children of limited English proficiency (1978). This is important because proficiency is broader than speaking ability and implies that children should not be exited from programs based on speaking ability alone. The 1984 reauthorization included provisions for family English literacy programs for families of children served and for developmental (two-way) bilingual programs.

Expansions of Title VII have provided funding for a wide range of activities associated with dual language instruction. Basic services to children, preservice and in-service training for teachers and trainers of teachers, research activities, program evaluation, and nationwide dissemination of information on bilingual education are all funded through Title VII.

Most recently, on October 20, 1994, President Bill Clinton signed Public Law 103-382, Improving America's Schools Act of 1994, which reauthorized the Elementary and Secondary Education Act of 1965, including Title VII, "Bilingual Education, Language Enhancement, and Language Acquisition Programs."

This fifth reauthorization of Title VII provides funding on a competitive, discretionary basis. Funds for direct services to students are available in the following categories:

- *program development and implementation grants:* three-year grants for the development and implementation of new bilingual programs
- *enhancement grants:* two-year grants for the improvement and expansion of existing programs
- *comprehensive school grants:* five-year grants to support reform and restructuring aimed at improving services of all limited English proficient students in a school
- *comprehensive district grants:* five-year grants aimed at meeting the needs of limited English proficient students by upgrading programs K–12

Along with basic programs, the act addresses professional development and includes the following components:

- *training for all teachers program:* five-year grants to train pre- and inservice teachers in the strategies and methods all teachers need to best serve limited English proficient students
- *bilingual education teachers and personnel grants:* five-year grants to support bilingual teacher training
- *bilingual education career ladder program:* five-year grants for programs designed to assist paraprofessionals in obtaining the training necessary for certification as teachers
- *graduate fellowships in bilingual education program:* grants to support students engaged in masters, doctoral, or post-doctoral work related to meeting the educational needs of limited English proficient students

To support the improvement of instructional services for limited English proficient students, the act supports research, program evaluation, and dissemination of information. As in the past, funding is provided for a National Clearinghouse for Bilingual Education, as well as for regional technical assistance centers.

The act now provides discretionary funding to support districts that have large influxes of immigrant students. In addition, the newly reauthorized act provides funding for the establishment, improvement, or expansion of foreign language programs, K–12. Pressure groups and legislators opposed to bilingual education have made repeated attempts to block each reauthorization or to alter the act substantially, minimizing or eliminating primary language instruction. However, these attempts have met with little success. By linking bilingual education to the school reform movement and by creating conceptual linkages between bilingual and foreign language instruction, the 1994 reauthorization opens the door to broad-based support for dual language instruction.

## Discretionary Funding

Some forms of government funding are available to individuals who are members of a defined class. For example, Chapter 1 support for academic assistance is available from the government for any child who meets the established academic and income criteria. Other forms of government funding are not automatically available to defined classes of people, but are awarded on a competitive basis. Title VII, for example, does not require dual language instruction for every student who is limited English proficient, nor does it provide monetary assistance for every individual who qualifies.

Instead, local school districts, universities, or state agencies may apply for Title VII funds by submitting a grant application to the federal government. Applicants must describe the proposed program, indicate the need for it, describe the qualifications of the personnel involved, and provide an evaluation plan.

The funding process is competitive; thus, not all applicants receive funding. Title VII is intended to help educational agencies to establish mechanisms for delivering services for limited English proficient students that will then become part of the agency's regularly funded and supported activities.

## Title VII Sets Policy

Title VII does not mandate dual language instruction for all students or any students. Such a mandate would be out of keeping with the federal role in education. Title VII does, however, set national policy regarding services for children who are limited English proficient. It does so in two ways.

The first is through legislative language. The act acknowledges that there are large numbers of children who would benefit from instruction in their primary language using bilingual educational methods and techniques and goes on to say:

> Congress declares it to be the policy of the United States, in order to establish equal educational opportunity for all children, to encourage the establishment and operation, where appropriate, of educational programs using bilingual educational practices, techniques, and methods. . . .

The second way Title VII influences policy is through infrastructure. Title VII funding provides for the establishment of basic programs and also supports training for school personnel in the area of dual language instruction. In addition, money provided for basic research and program evaluation allows educators to develop the theory and methodology necessary to properly serve children in dual language programs. National networking disseminates information, making it possible for educational agencies to benefit from each other's experiments and expertise. To the extent that funding permits, programs, training, and research can result in a knowledge and advocacy base that creates a solid infrastructure for dual language education.

## LAU v. NICHOLS (1974)

As mentioned above, the U.S. Supreme Court has played a decisive role in many areas of education, and dual language instruction is no exception. In 1969, plaintiffs representing 1,800 language minority children in the San Francisco Unified School District sued the district, claiming that limited English proficient children were being denied equal educational opportunity in English-only classrooms.

Overturning the decision of a lower court, the Supreme Court decided in favor of the plaintiffs under Title VI of the Civil Rights Act. The language in the decision was strong. Justice William O. Douglas wrote:

> There is no equality of treatment merely by providing students with the same facilities, textbooks, teachers, and curriculum; for students who do not understand English are effectively foreclosed from any meaningful education. Basic skills are at the very core of what these public schools teach. Imposition of a requirement that, before a child can effectively participate in the educational program he must already have acquired those basic skills is to make a mockery of public education. We know that those who do not understand English are certain to find their classroom experiences wholly incomprehensible and in no way meaningful.

### Interpretation of Lau

The Court held for the plaintiffs in the *Lau* decision, and the case undoubtedly represents a victory for the rights of language minority children. There are several points, however, which should be borne in mind when considering *Lau* and its effects.

The *Lau* decision was an interpretation of the Civil Rights Act. At the time the Supreme Court agreed to review *Lau*, they refused to review *Serna v. Portales* (1974), a similar case that was argued on the basis of the equal protection clause of the Constitution. In deciding *Lau*, the Court avoided the constitutional issue. A decision on constitutional grounds would have been stronger than the decision rendered on the basis of a statute. This is true because Congress could make *Lau* irrelevant by simply passing a different law. In contrast, a constitutional amendment would be necessary to overturn a Supreme Court decision interpreting the Constitution.

Another issue that was raised by the case was numbers. In his concurring opinion in the *Lau* case, Justice Harry A. Blackmun observed that for him numbers were "at the heart of this case," suggesting that he might have viewed the situation differently if smaller numbers of children had been involved.

Finally, it should be noted that in deciding *Lau* the Court did not specify any particular remedy. The Court held that districts failing to provide services for children who could not function in English were violating the civil rights of those children. And it did require that San Francisco Unified School District take affirmative steps to eliminate the inequities suffered by limited English proficient children as a result of its policies. But there is no requirement in *Lau* that districts must establish bilingual programs.

## Effects of *Lau*

The *Lau* decision had several dramatic and immediate effects. In 1975 the Department of Health, Education, and Welfare (HEW) and the Office of Civil Rights (OCR) of the federal government developed a document to provide districts with guidance for implementing programs in compliance with Title VI of the Civil Rights Act as interpreted in *Lau*. The document, known as the "*Lau* Remedies," established standards for identifying limited English speaking children, assessing their language ability, and meeting their needs. The *Lau* Remedies were never formally accorded regulatory status, but did serve as the basis for compliance reviews by the Office of Civil Rights, which meant that districts generally attempted to abide by the requirements in the document.

*Lau* had an impact on other court cases that were pending at the time. In New York, for example, Aspira, a Puerto Rican community group, had filed suit against the New York City Board of Education on behalf of the system's approximately 182,000 Spanish-speaking students (*Aspira of New York, Inc. v. Board of Education,* 1972). Shortly after *Lau* was decided, the parties to the suit entered into a consent decree in which the New York City Board of Education agreed to provide substantial bilingual services to children of limited English ability.

Also, soon after *Lau* a number of states, including California and Texas, passed laws mandating some form of bilingual education (McFadden, 1983). While *Lau* did not require any specific remedy or form of program, it favored the establishment of bilingual programs as a way of avoiding civil rights violations.

Advocates for the rights of language minority children have begun, in recent years, to rely less on *Lau* and instead based their arguments on the Equal Educational Opportunities Act of 1974, which is more specific than *Lau*.

## EQUAL EDUCATIONAL OPPORTUNITIES ACT OF 1974

Section 1703(f) of the Equal Educational Opportunities Act (EEOA) states:

No state shall deny equal educational opportunity to an individual on account of his or her race, color, sex, or national origin by . . . (f) the failure by an educational agency to take appropriate action to overcome language barriers that impede equal participation by its students in its instructional programs.

Section 1703(f) of EEOA restates the underlying principle of the *Lau* decision in statutory form. There is a growing body of federal case law that interprets the statute (*Castañeda v. Pickard,* 1981; *Keyes v. School District No. 1,* 1983; *Gomez v. Illinois,* 1987; *Idaho Migrant Council v. Board,* 1981). The cases do not require bilingual education but they do require equal access to the curriculum. In other words, children may not sit in classrooms where they cannot understand what is going on. Affirmative steps must be taken to ensure that all children have a meaningful educational experience. As articulated in the case law, in order to properly serve students who are limited English proficient, districts must:

- develop a program based on a sound theoretical rationale
- provide trained teachers and sufficient material resources to implement the program
- develop an evaluation system for the program and refine the program in accordance with information from the evaluation

Federal law protecting the rights of language minority children is of particular importance in areas where states have weakened or eliminated their own requirements regarding bilingual education. Under federal law, children who lack sufficient English skills to succeed in English-only classrooms are entitled to an educational opportunity equal to that of their English-speaking peers.

## STATE LAWS REGARDING BILINGUAL EDUCATION

Prior to *Lau,* the only state-mandated dual language program in the United States was in Massachusetts. Massachusetts's vanguard bilingual education law required a transitional program if 20 or more children in a school district on the same grade level were limited English proficient and had the same primary language. Many other states, to the contrary, required by law that instruction be delivered in English. The passage of the federal Bilingual Education Act in 1968 had a positive effect on the political climate regarding dual language instruction, but funded only a relative handful of programs to meet the needs of children with limited English abilities.

By the mid-1980s, twenty states had bilingual education requirements. The majority of those laws, however, require programs that are transitional and compensatory in nature. This is unfortunate, because compensatory programs are perceived by the general public as peripheral. Without wide popular support, dual language programs are often at risk, especially since the population they currently attempt to serve is often disenfranchised by its lack of English proficiency. Two-way programs offering second language skills to all students are more likely to build a broader political base, but such programs are relatively rare.

The future of state mandated bilingual education is insecure at the present time. Illinois repealed its statute in 1980 but reinstated it under community pressure. California, with a school enrollment of over a million limited English proficient children, has allowed its legislation to lapse. Florida, on the other hand, had no state mandate for serving LEP students until 1990. Following a lawsuit initiated by a coalition of advocacy groups, that state entered into a consent decree that outlines a plan for identifying and serving its sizable LEP student population. Federal protections of the rights of limited English proficient students are still in effect, however, and in the face of increasing needs, communities will undoubtedly use them to support dual language instructional programming.


## BILINGUAL EDUCATION AND DESEGREGATION

There is a perception among some professionals and community members that bilingual education and desegregation are incompatible as means of providing equal educational opportunity for minority students. This misconception arises for several reasons.

School desegregation has been strongly identified with the conflicts between black and white communities, and resolution of the issues has not always included a discussion of the needs of Hispanic or other minority and language minority groups. In fact, there have been instances where Hispanic students have been sadly exploited in the battle for desegregated schools. After the *Brown* decision for example, Mexican American students in Texas who were categorized as whites were used to "desegregate" black schools, thereby avoiding true desegregation (Weinberg, 1977).

Also, desegregation often takes the form of student reassignment and busing, which dilutes the concentration of limited English proficient children in any one school. In order to create coherent bilingual programs it is necessary to group limited English proficient students in sufficient numbers to create whole classes —preferably classes on several consecutive grade levels. In fact, state bilingual education laws generally require a given number of limited English proficient students to "trigger" a bilingual classroom. Dispersing students through reassignment limits bilingual services in those situations.

In addition, desegregation usually includes reassignment of staff. Teachers with bilingual competency are often members of minority groups. Desegregation plans that include assignment of minority teachers to majority schools or classes may result in the denial of services to limited English proficient children, especially since bilingual teachers are in extremely short supply.

The perception that bilingual education is in conflict with desegregation was heightened by a federal court decision in *Keyes v. School District No. 1* (1975), in which the court held that court-ordered desegregation precluded a bilingual maintenance program. In Boston, however, a desegregation plan ordered by the Massachusetts federal district court included steps to preserve the integrity of established bilingual programs by clustering limited English proficient students as part of the reassignment process (*Morgan v. Kerrigan*, 1975).

Desegregation plans need not dismantle bilingual programs. Limited English proficient children need not be randomly assigned in order to desegregate schools. Moreover, bilingual programs themselves need not be segregated. Two-way bilingual programs have gained popularity as "magnets," special programming to attract white children to predominantly nonwhite schools. Through innovative curricula that promote bilingualism and cross-cultural understanding, two-way programs can transcend desegregation, creating the opportunity for integration and equal educational opportunity for all children.

## SUMMARY

Legislative and judicial support for publicly funded dual language instructional programs is rooted historically in the civil rights movement. Support at the federal level resides in legislation that provides funding for bilingual programs, civil rights legislation, and case law that requires that limited English proficient students be served. Many states have laws requiring some form of dual language instruction for students who need it, but two-way programming rarely receives legislative support, and the future of requirements for bilingual education at the state level is uncertain at the present time.

There is a concern among some advocates of dual language instruction that desegregation plans will dilute or dismantle services for limited English proficient students. The needs of limited English proficient children can be met in desegregation plans. Furthermore, such plans may offer an opportunity for the implementation of two-way bilingual programs serving both language minority and majority populations.

## ACTIVITIES AND QUESTIONS TO THINK ABOUT

1. Speak to the person in your local school district who is in charge of federally funded projects. How much federal money does the district receive annually? What kinds of activities are funded by federal dollars?

2. Find out if your local school district or university receives Title VII funds. Speak to the people who developed the project proposal. Find out what they included in their application and what difficulties they encountered in preparing it. What kind of project are they funded for, and how much money do they receive?

3. Does your state have a bilingual education statute? What kinds of programs are mandated? How are they implemented?

# THE LEARNING GAME

OFFICE: 408-996-8064
FAX: 408-996-8065
20540 STEVENS CREEK BLVD.
CUPERTINO, CA 95014

## SUGGESTIONS FOR FURTHER READING

Readings on the legal foundations of bilingual education are difficult to identify, since statutes, court cases, and their interpretations are generally available in formats appropriate for legal professionals, while failing to meet the needs of lay readers. The books suggested below have chapters devoted to the topic. The articles mentioned have in-depth legal analyses of related issues. Statutes can be changed and court decisions can alter interpretations at any time; therefore, the reader is cautioned that information of this kind can quickly become obsolete.

Ambert, A. N., & Melendez, S. E. (1985). *Bilingual education: A sourcebook.* New York: Teachers College Press.
This book covers a wide range of issues related to bilingual education and should be considered a basic resource for the field. The chapter on legal issues includes an analysis of several cases that were decided after *Lau,* and the annotated bibliography will be useful to readers interested in studying legal issues in greater depth.

Castellanos, D. (1983). *The best of two worlds: Bilingual-bicultural education in the U.S.* Trenton, NJ: New Jersey State Department of Education.
Already reviewed in Chapter 4 for its history of dual language instruction, this book deserves further attention for its detailed analysis of the legal status of dual language instruction in historical context. While the book does not predate the Equal Educational Opportunities Act, it was published before the implications of the EEOA were evident.

LaFontaine, H., Persky, B., & Golubchick, L. H. (1978). *Bilingual education.* Wayne, NJ: Avery.
A collection of readings on a wide variety of topics related to bilingual education, this book contains a section devoted to legal issues. Ten years have elapsed since this book was published, and there has, of course, been new legislation and litigation in that time. These articles, however, contain valuable information for the student who wants to investigate this area.

McFadden, B. J. (1983). Bilingual education and the law. *Journal of Law & Education, 12,* 1–27.
This article focuses on federal litigation and its impact on bilingual education. The analysis of *Lau* and its weaknesses are clear and accessible to the lay reader and provide the groundwork for understanding the importance of subsequent legislation and litigation.

Nieto, S. (Ed.). (1986). Bilingual education and equity. Special issue. *Interracial Books for Children Bulletin, 17* (3 & 4).
The objective of this special issue of *Bulletin* is to provide information about bilingual education and equity, generally only available in specialized publications, to a wider public. In addition to readings on the educational rationale for dual language instruction, the publication contains articles about legal issues and desegregation.

Teitelbaum, H., & Hiller, R. J. (1977). Bilingual education: The legal mandate. *Harvard Educational Review, 47,* 138–170.
This article provides a detailed analysis of *Lau* and subsequent federal cases, along with an analysis of obstacles to bilingual education that may not be quickly altered by litigation.

chapter **11**

# The Politics of Bilingualism

$\mathbf{I}$n preceding chapters we have considered language and culture and have built an educational rationale to support primary language instruction for limited English proficient students and second language enrichment for monolingual English speakers. While we have generally emphasized the benefits of dual language instruction for individual students, schooling exists within a large social and political framework. When we make decisions about language use in public school classrooms, we are also implementing government-sponsored language policy. This chapter will discuss language policy and how governments can promote or suppress languages.

Current population changes in the United States have provoked reactions to immigration that are often couched in some form of language resistance. This chapter will describe U.S. language policies and how costly and dangerous it can be to resist multilingualism, dual language instruction, and modern or foreign language learning.

Popular conceptions of our national identity determine the context in which language policy and language resistance come into existence. The chapter will conclude with a discussion of assimilationism, the relationship between assimilationism and pluralism, and the role of schooling in promoting a positive multicultural vision in the United States.

## LANGUAGE POLICY AND PLANNING

Shirley Brice Heath (1983), a prominent sociolinguist, defines language policies as "what the government says and does through its laws, legislative statutes, regulations, and bureaucratic practices that affect the choices and uses of one or more languages used by the people it represents (p. 156)." Sometimes a nation's policy is stated in the form of recognition of official languages, either through legislation or in a national constitution. At other times, language policy is established by legislation and regulation of language use in courts, schools, and other government agencies, or through a government body such as a language academy. Through language policies, it is possible for governments to promote minority languages or to suppress them.

## Language Support

Language support includes graphization, or the creation of a writing system; standardization or the creation of an orthography and grammar; modernization or expansion of the vocabulary; and dissemination—usually through teacher training and support in the schools.

The University of Hawaii, for example, with the support of the government of the Trust Territory of the Pacific Islands, has provided support for the languages of the Trust Territories (now the independent countries of the Federated States of Micronesia, the Republic of Belau, the Commonwealth of the Marianas, and the Marshall Islands). The university's support for local languages has included the development of orthographies, the publication of dictionaries and grammars, and teacher training to support dissemination of orthographies and to encourage primary language literacy in schools.

Language planning strategies are easy to formulate on paper. In practice, however, they are complicated by historical and social factors. In the case of the Trust Territories, for example, new orthographies are difficult to establish. Except for the Bible, published in vernaculars by missionaries, there was little printed matter in local languages prior to World War II. Old habits die hard, and the old-fashioned printing methods still in use in these remote areas are cumbersome to retool for new writing systems.

New writing systems are difficult to disseminate for other reasons. After a century of colonial domination by a series of foreign powers, teachers in the Pacific islands have internalized the idea that primary languages should not be used for instruction, and they associate modernization and economic success with the use of English. While some teachers have become convinced that primary language instruction is valuable, materials in local languages are limited. Basic instructional materials have been created in local languages, but the development of primary language literacy skills is hindered by the fact that local languages generally have oral traditions. There is, for example, no backlog of written children's literature as we know it in English, and teachers cannot easily find children's books to supplement skills development.

Since its inception as a field 20 years ago, language planning has broadened its purview beyond approaches to standardization and dissemination. Language planning specialists have begun to consider language problems and solutions and to develop strategies for managing language change within the context of the historical, social, economic, and political circumstances of a nation (Eastman, 1983).

## Language Suppression

It is possible for a government to suppress a minority language in a number of ways. Governments can ban the use of minority languages in the media and in public life. Basque, for example, was vehemently suppressed during the Franco regime in Spain but has been restored to the status of an official provincial language under the current liberal monarchy (Grosjean, 1982).

Another way to suppress a minority language is to promote the idea that it is a substandard dialect of a majority language. Catalan, the language of Catalonia in northeastern Spain, is similar to Spanish in several ways, but linguists and speakers alike agree that Spanish and Catalan are different languages. Catalonia resisted the Franco regime, and, in an attempt to silence Catalonian resistance, Franco's government deemed Catalan a dialect and made attempts to eradicate it. Catalan was restored to the status of an official language after Franco's death, and a provincial government agency was established to stimulate its reinstitution (Woolard, 1985). Interestingly, the local government has recently tried to impose Catalan as the only language of instruction in the schools as an attempt to undo the damage done under Franco's rule. The new policy has angered some Spanish-speaking parents of school children, who have gone to court to block the government's implementation of it (Battle in Spain, 1993).

It has long been recognized that one potent way to suppress a particular language is to establish laws or policies forbidding its use in schools. Examples of this practice are numerous. During the Spanish colonial period in Latin America, missionaries were directed to provide instruction for Indians in Castilian, in an attempt to replace indigenous languages (Weinberg, 1977). During the Japanese colonial period in the Pacific islands between World Wars I and II, schooling was compulsory and all instruction was delivered in Japanese.

United States colonial policies have included attempts to use schools as a tool for replacing local languages with English in Hawaii, the Philippines, and Puerto Rico. Replacement of American Indian languages through forced schooling played a significant role in debilitating American Indian societies and destroying indigenous North American cultures.

The use of Spanish in the United States has traditionally provoked repressive reactions. Spanish is indigenous to the Southwest, and its continued use there is supported by substantial and continuing immigration by Spanish speakers. Our proximity to Mexico and a thousand miles of border make Spanish a viable southwestern language. On the East Coast, there are large numbers of Puerto Ricans who are citizens by birth and native Spanish speakers. The United States is the logical destination for Spanish-speaking refugees and immigrants from all of Latin America and the Caribbean. As a result, Spanish is widely spoken in the

United States and seems to have staying power. There have been rigorous and ongoing attempts to suppress the use of Spanish in schools, including ridiculing, punishing, and expelling children for speaking it, even in play (Carter, 1970).

## LANGUAGE RESISTANCE IN THE UNITED STATES

In Chapter 1 we described how multilingualism and the use of more than one language in the schools have been part of our national heritage since before colonial times. But the American experience has included resistance to cultural and linguistic diversity as well.

Language resistance includes language parochialism, the attitude that multilingualism is not useful and may even be harmful, and language elitism, the attitude that bilingualism is desirable for individuals of elevated status but unacceptable for members of ethnic minority groups. Parochialism and elitism are costly—both economically and politically—and they set the stage for restrictionism. *Language restrictionism* is the attempt to formally promulgate a language policy by imposing restrictions on language use.

Movements to restrict language use reach beyond the education system and are tied into large political and social issues. Language restrictionism in the United States has generally accompanied anti-immigration movements. As a result, restrictionist movements flourished at the end of the nineteenth century and are gaining popularity at the present time. Dual language teachers and advocates need to be aware of the dynamics of language parochialism, elitism, and restrictionism since they may have significant impacts on dual language education; conversely, dual language instruction may be an important tool in combating language resistance.

## Language Parochialism

Language parochialism might be characterized as an attitude about language that holds multilingualism in low regard and fails to acknowledge the benefits of language sophistication. In 1980 Paul Simon, at that time a congressman from Illinois, wrote a book titled *The Tongue-Tied American,* which details the effects of language parochialism. In the book's preface, the author asserts that he is "not a language expert," but in his book he has collected information about Americans and languages that is of serious concern to us all. According to Simon, American resistance to language learning and negative attitudes about bilingualism are costly to our nation, both economically and politically. American monolingualism may be damaging, for example, in the following areas.

*International Trade.*    It is common wisdom that you can buy in any language but you should sell in the language of your customer. Around the world, sales people are expected to be multilingual. U.S. business people, however, generally expect to conduct business in English, and our monolingualism and lack of cultural sensitivity has damaged our viability in the international marketplace. Simon (1980) has cataloged some of our more embarrassing attempts to advertise in foreign markets:

"'Body by Fisher', describing a General Motors product, came out 'Corpse by Fisher' in Flemish. . . . Schweppes Tonic was advertised in Italy as 'bathroom water.' . . . 'Come Alive With Pepsi' almost appeared in the Chinese version of the *Reader's Digest* as 'Pepsi brings your ancestors back from the grave'" (p. 32).

Translation errors are amusing, but these examples demonstrate not only a lack of ability in particular languages but a lack of knowledge about languages in general and about the relationships between languages and culture. In a special report prepared during the Carter administration, the President's Commission on Foreign Language and International Studies commented:

> International trade involves one out of every eight of America's manu-
> facturing jobs and one out of every three acres of America's farmland.
> . . . If the U.S. is to export more and compete more effectively in inter-
> national trade, it is the many small and middle-level firms that must be
> involved. . . . But American business people at these levels are often at
> a disadvantage when functioning internationally. They rarely speak
> foreign languages and have little experience or cultural skills in negoti-
> ating with foreign enterprises or governments. (*Strength through
> Wisdom,* 1979, p. 47)

An article in *Fortune* (Kirkland, 1988) declares: "Thinking about going global? Friend, you're too late. The train has already left. Today the competition for goods, services, and ideas pays no respects to national borders. . . ." (p. 40). The article enumerates the business rules of today's "global village."

- Every imaginable kind of product is produced and marketed on a worldwide basis.
- Even if you only market in the United States, you will face foreign competition.
- Overseas corporations may not choose to compete with U.S. businesses. They may buy them instead.
- Successful U.S. businesses have stopped thinking of global markets strictly as consumers and consider them as suppliers, not only of products but of technology.
- Successful U.S. businesses not only compete with foreign counterparts; they cooperate with them to improve products, technology, and profits.

Kirkland concludes:

> Even if you run a drugstore in Knoxville . . . you still need to cultivate
> a more planetary planning horizon. The cost of the merchandise you

sell, the sales pitches that captivate your customers, even the price of your mortgage and the size of your tax bite, increasingly reflect the exotic influence of decisions made on the Tokyo stock exchange or launched over lunch by London admen. (pp. 40, 42)

From the largest corporation to the local pharmacy, our linguistic and cultural deficiencies become more costly as we become more involved in an interdependent global economy.

***National Security.***    During World War II, the military recognized the need for personnel with skills in foreign languages as essential to our national defense. As we discussed in Chapter 7, the U.S. Army took a leadership role in developing innovative language teaching strategies. After the war, the National Defense Education Act (1958) provided financial assistance to stimulate foreign language study. Funding for the act continued for a decade, and during that period of support, enrollment in high school foreign language courses in the United States increased from 16.5 to 27.7 percent (Benderson, 1983). Unfortunately, in the decades following the act, national interest in the study of foreign languages declined (see Table 11.1), and our monolingualism has hampered our national security efforts.

For example, during the revolution in Iran in 1978 only 6 of the 60 U.S. Foreign Service officers assigned there were Farsi speakers (Kondracke, 1979). As you may remember, anti-American feeling in Iran escalated to monumental proportions that year, culminating in a situation where 53 American embassy personnel were held hostage for nearly a year. According to Simon (1980), only one of the 120 journalists assigned to Iran during the hostage crisis spoke Farsi.

Americans often assume that everyone speaks English. English is widely used as the language of science and commerce and is the language most used as a second language around the world (Ferguson, 1978). Widespread use of English may facilitate your shopping on a pleasure trip. It is unlikely, however, that you would be able to take the measure of a sensitive political situation in a foreign country using only English.

English speakers in non-English-speaking countries are likely to be members of a country's educated elite and may therefore be incapable of properly assessing the total political climate in which they live. Also, intelligence gathered in English or translated may be inaccurate, lacking in significant cultural and social nuances. The Iranian situation is but one instance where our lack of language resources has placed us in a politically dangerous situation.

Recently, there has been renewed interest in foreign language instruction at the elementary level (Viadero, 1991). For example, the state of Oregon, as part of its statewide school reform efforts, has enacted mastery standards that require students to demonstrate proficiency in a second language by the 10th grade (Graves & Rubenstein, 1995). Colleges have reported a growth in enrollment in Spanish language classes, although enrollment in French and German has declined (Cage, 1994). As we have already seen, however, language learning takes time. Also, much as any individual's language learning is enhanced by a positive social climate, programs require a supportive policy climate in order to succeed. Support for language teaching and learning have not consistently been part of the American educational system.

## Language Elitism

In the United States, bilingualism has often been viewed with disfavor. This is particularly wasteful given that we have large numbers of people within our borders who speak languages other than English and who could serve as language resources to our entire nation.

Yet our attitudes toward bilingualism are ambivalent. We consider it a worthwhile accomplishment for a college graduate from an English-speaking background to master a second language. But we insist that the children of immigrant families relinquish their first languages as part of their Americanization. Kjolseth (1983) has suggested that we tend to admire individual bilinguals, such as celebrities, scholars, and diplomats, and to disparage group bilinguals, or members of ethnic groups. In the popular view, individual bilingualism is often associated with elevated socioeconomic status; group bilingualism is generally associated with poverty and lack of education. Individual bilinguals acquire their second language through effort and scholarship; group bilinguals acquire their second language at home.

An eighth-grade student from a family of migrant farmworkers in Colorado told me, "I like school better here than in Texas. In Texas they punished me for speaking Spanish in school. The white kids were learning Spanish and tried to practice with us, but when we answered them we got punished." We fail to recognize that bilingualism is valuable regardless of its source.

*Hunger of Memory* (Rodriguez, 1982), the autobiography of a Mexican American writer and scholar, received much attention when it was published, because the author suggested that giving up Spanish was a first and essential step on his road to Americanization. Opponents of dual language instruction hailed the book and pointed to the author's experiences as proof positive that English monolingualism leads to successful assimilation. But a persistently apologetic and yearning tone underlies Rodriguez's autobiography, leading the reader to question his assertion that giving up Spanish was necessary and positive in establishing his identity as a North American.

Einar Haugen (1987), a bilingual Norwegian American sociolinguist, observed:

> The loss of the mother tongue in home and church could be a bitter experience. It is well known that a second language learned in later life often fails to convey the cultural, emotional, or religious power of the first language, the mother tongue. Even with my entire schooling in English, my Norwegian background somehow makes a Norwegian poem or quotation warmer and more deeply moving than its English equivalent (p. 24).

**TABLE 11.1** Enrollment in foreign language courses (grades 9–12, United States, fall 1948 to fall 1982, in thousands)

| Language<br>1 | Fall<br>1948<br>2 | Fall<br>1960<br>3 | Fall<br>1965<br>4 | Fall<br>1968<br>5 | Fall<br>1970<br>6 | Fall<br>1974<br>7 | Fall<br>1976<br>8 | Fall<br>1978<br>9 | Fall<br>1982<br>10 | Percentage Change in Enrollment | |
|---|---|---|---|---|---|---|---|---|---|---|---|
| | | | | | | | | | | 1965 to<br>1970<br>11 | 1970 to<br>1982<br>12 |
| Total enrollment, grades 9 to 12 | 5,602[1] | 8,589 | 11,610 | 12,718 | 13,332 | 14,132 | 14,311 | 14,223 | 12,496 | 14.8 | −6.3 |
| All foreign languages[2] | | | | | | | | | | | |
| Number enrolled | 1,170 | 2,522 | 3,659 | 3,890 | 3,779 | 3,295 | 3,174 | 3,048 | 2,910 | 3.3 | −23.0 |
| Percentage of all students | 20.9 | 29.4 | 31.5 | 30.6 | 28.3 | 23.3 | 22.2 | 21.4 | 23.3 | — | — |
| Modern foreign languages | | | | | | | | | | | |
| Number enrolled | 741 | 1,867 | 3,068 | 3,518 | 3,514 | 3,127 | 3,023 | 2,897 | 2,740 | 14.6 | −22.0 |
| Percentage of all students | 13.2 | 21.7 | 26.4 | 27.7 | 26.4 | 22.1 | 21.1 | 20.4 | 21.9 | — | — |
| Spanish | | | | | | | | | | | |
| Number enrolled | 443 | 933 | 1,427 | 1,698 | 1,811 | 1,678 | 1,717 | 1,631 | 1,563 | 26.9 | −13.7 |
| Percentage of all students | 7.9 | 10.9 | 12.3 | 13.4 | 13.6 | 11.9 | 12.0 | 11.5 | 12.5 | — | — |
| French | | | | | | | | | | | |
| Number enrolled | 254 | 744 | 1,251 | 1,328 | 1,231 | 978 | 888 | 856 | 858 | −1.7 | −30.3 |
| Percentage of all students | 4.5 | 8.7 | 10.8 | 10.4 | 9.2 | 6.9 | 6.2 | 6.0 | 6.9 | — | — |

|  | | | | | | | | | | | |
|---|---|---|---|---|---|---|---|---|---|---|---|
| **German** | | | | | | | | | | | |
| Number enrolled | 43 | 151 | 328 | 423 | 411 | 393 | 353 | 331 | 267 | 25.2 | −35.0 |
| Percentage of all students | 0.8 | 1.8 | 2.8 | 3.3 | 3.1 | 2.8 | 2.5 | 2.3 | 2.1 | — | — |
| **Russian** | | | | | | | | | | | |
| Number enrolled | — | 10 | 27 | 24 | 20 | 15 | 11 | 9 | 6 | −24.5 | −71.7 |
| Percentage of all students | — | 0.1 | 0.2 | 0.2 | 0.2 | 0.1 | 0.1 | 0.1 | (3) | — | — |
| **Italian** | | | | | | | | | | | |
| Number enrolled | — | 20 | 25 | 27 | 27 | 46 | 46 | 46 | 44 | 8.3 | 61.5 |
| Percentage of all students | — | 0.2 | 0.2 | 0.2 | 0.2 | 0.3 | 0.3 | 0.3 | 0.4 | — | — |
| **Other modern foreign languages** | | | | | | | | | | | |
| Number enrolled | 1 | 9 | 9 | 18 | 15 | 23 | 9 | 24 | 3 | 54.4 | −81.4 |
| Percentage of all students | (3) | 0.1 | 0.1 | 0.1 | 0.1 | 0.2 | 0.1 | 0.2 | (3) | — | — |
| **Latin** | | | | | | | | | | | |
| Number enrolled | 429 | 655 | 591 | 372 | 265 | 167 | 150 | 152 | 170 | −55.1 | −36.1 |
| Percentage of all students | 7.7 | 7.6 | 5.1 | 2.9 | 2.0 | 1.2 | 1.1 | 1.1 | 1.4 | — | — |

NOTE: Some data have been revised slightly from previously published figures. Because of rounding, details may not add to totals.
[1]Estimated.
[2]Includes enrollment in ancient Greek (not shown separately). Fewer than 1,000 students were enrolled in this language in each of the years shown.
[3]Less than 0.05 percent. Blank indicates data not reported, not available, or not applicable.
SOURCE: *Digest of Education Statistics 1987.* Washington, DC: Center for Education Statistics.

American attitudes toward language study are not shared around the world. Simon's survey of foreign school systems (1980, pp. 77-90) indicates that required study of two or more languages is common outside the United States, even in developing nations, where resources may be scarce. The *New York Times* reports that even in France, where students traditionally have studied a foreign language at the secondary level, recognition of the need to know several languages in an increasingly unified political and economic environment has led to the introduction of foreign languages in the primary grades (Riding, 1992). And an informal survey in my own classrooms each semester reveals that, unlike students educated in the United States, students educated in Asia, Latin America, and the Middle East almost always were required to study at least one foreign language as a matter of course. (See Chapter 4 for a discussion of dual language instruction in other countries.)

Elitist attitudes about bilingualism cause us to squander our linguistic resources. One can only wonder how many children enter schools in the United States where the use of their first language is discouraged or even punished, only to enroll in high school foreign language classes to try to recapture some of their lost language wealth. Entrenched in English monolingualism, we fail to acknowledge our multilingualism as a national resource, limit our ability to trade on world markets, and endanger our security as a nation.

## Language Restrictionism

Today's fast-moving social and political changes have evoked predictable reaction and resistance. One form this resistance has taken is language restrictionism, the attempt to limit language use through government policy. Language restrictionism is not new in the United States, but it is currently enjoying a renaissance and may have devastating effects both on our education systems and on our political and economic success as a nation.

***Historical Perspectives.***   As we saw in Chapter 8, our history is characterized by immigration, and immigration invariably has been met by reactionary movements designed to limit the arrival of newcomers. Such reactionary movements usually include a component directed at language use, which serves as a thin veil to obscure the bigotry they espouse.

Schools are often the scene of the first interactions between an incoming group and the public sphere; thus, language restrictionist movements invariably mount an attack on the use of languages other than English in the schools. Current language restrictionists focus on Spanish, which they find particularly threatening. The strategies and arguments they use, however, are not new and have been directed at other groups in the past. As we saw earlier, German and English coexisted comfortably for most of the nineteenth century. At first, attacks on German were a byproduct of reactions directed at incoming Irish immigrants, but the advent of World War I brought anti-German feeling to hysterical proportions.

Through the courts, German Americans were able to protect the use of German for instruction from political attack, but from a practical point of view, the damage was done. German school systems were seriously debilitated, and the numbers of students receiving German instruction declined.

Language restrictionist sentiment spread to include all languages other than English, and several states passed laws restricting instruction in schools to the English language. The state of Nebraska attempted to limit foreign language instruction to high schools, but in 1923 the United States Supreme Court held in *Meyer v. Nebraska* that the prohibition of the use or teaching of a foreign language was unconstitutional.

***Language Restrictionism in the Present.*** As we have seen, there has been an increase in immigration and in the diversity of newcomers in the 1980s. Current anti-immigrationists support an English-only agenda as part of their efforts to resist population change. The primary agenda of the English-only movement is a constitutional amendment making English the official language nationwide. While this idea has met with significant and appropriate resistance on the part of federal lawmakers, 12 states passed legislation or constitutional amendments between 1983 and 1988 declaring English their official language, bringing the total to 14 (Perez, 1988). In 1994, however, the U.S. Court of Appeals for the Ninth Circuit upheld a federal district court ruling that held the Arizona English-only law in violation of Constitutional First Amendment protection of free speech (Contín, M., 1995).

Anti-immigrant sentiment is at the forefront of American politics. The passage of Proposition 187 in California, which bars illegal immigrants from receiving government services such as schooling and health care, has reignited and fueled the debate. The politics of immigration are invariably tied to language. Nevertheless, support for the English-only movement is far from unanimous. The cartoon in Figure 11.1 is an amusing but pointed reflection on language restrictionism in the United States.

***Voting.*** In 1975 Congress amended the Voting Rights Act to prohibit English-only elections and to require bilingual ballots in jurisdictions where the language minority population exceeds 5 percent and illiteracy rates exceed national norms. English-only advocates have targeted bilingual ballots and voting materials. In 1984, for example, California voters passed an initiative instructing the governor to inform Congress that California wanted to eliminate ballots in languages other than English. Supporters of the proposition no doubt felt that they were voting for assimilation. As legal scholar Kenneth Karst (1986) has observed, however: "Voting is not just an expression of political preferences; it is an assertion of belonging to a political community" (p. 347).

Encouraging people to vote, regardless of their English proficiency, encourages the assimilation process. Where bilingual ballots are used, ethnic minorities' participation in the political system has increased. New Mexico has had bilingual voting since it became a state in 1912, and it is the only state where the number

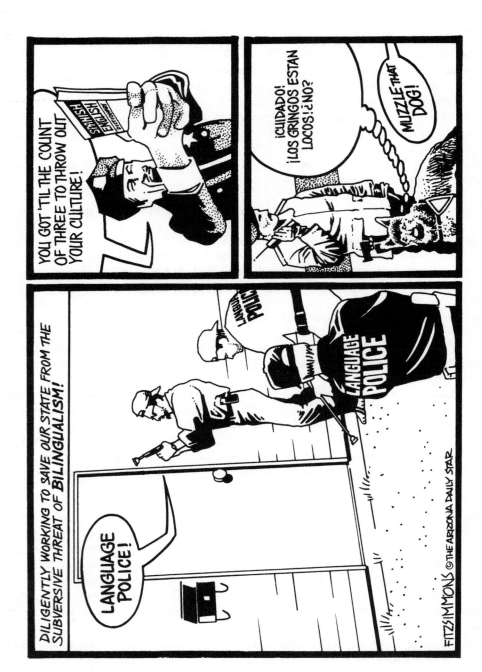

**FIGURE 11.1**  Language police cartoon

SOURCE: "Language Police," an editorial cartoon by David Fitzsimmons. *The Arizona Daily Star,* 1988. Reprinted with permission of *The Arizona Daily Star.*

of Hispanics in the state legislature is in proportion to their representation in the general population (Trasvina, 1981).

***Schooling.*** As part of their agenda, English-only proponents want to limit the time children spend in bilingual education programs. As we have seen, publicly funded bilingual programs focus on teaching English to limited English proficient children. As discussed in Chapter 6, research shows that the primary language is useful as an instructional bridge, and in addition, full development of two languages is beneficial to the education of any child. Furthermore, any educationally sound bilingual program model recognizes that second language learning takes time. Opponents of bilingual education commonly hold unrealistic and unsupported notions about how long it takes to learn a language well enough to compete with native speakers in a classroom.

***Language and Loyalty.*** Various minority groups during our history have suffered the suspicion of disloyalty. For example, in the nineteenth century, Catholics were often portrayed as maintaining a political allegiance to a foreign pope. More recently, the internment of people of Japanese ancestry during World War II is a terrifying example of the lengths to which fear and bigotry can carry us. A flier (see Box 11.1) was distributed in California during the campaign to make English the official state language. This flier, distributed by a group called U.S. ENGLISH, illustrates how language restrictionists equate language with loyalty and, frightened by our increasingly multicultural population, argue that multilingualism will lead to separatism and disunity. Proponents of language restrictionism often point to Canada, suggesting that support for two languages there has fueled national disunity and language segregation. They fail to acknowledge that much of the discord between minority French speakers and majority English speakers has dissipated since Canada has become officially bilingual.

Haugen (1987) points out the difference between horizontal and vertical bilingualism in social contexts. *Horizontal bilingualism* exists when different language groups enjoy equal status. Switzerland is an example of a horizontally bilingual environment. *Vertical bilingualism,* on the other hand, implies the domination of one language over another. Such vertical arrangements are far more volatile because of the social and political tensions that exist between the dominated and dominant groups. In Belgium for example, there has been ongoing strife between French speakers and Flemish speakers. French, a language of international status but the minority language in Belgium, continues to enjoy greater prestige than Flemish, the majority language, despite attempts by the federal government to dissipate the tension by treating both languages equally.

Separatism and language chauvinism flourish in the repressive environment of vertical bilingualism. Unity is born of mutual, horizontal tolerance and recognition.

***Outcomes.*** The fears of those who oppose the English-only movement have not been fully realized. In most areas, practical considerations require provisions for non-English speakers in schools, courts, hospitals, and social services. In the

---

### BOX 11.1   Language and Loyalty

*English, Our Common Bond*

Throughout its history, the United States has been enriched by the cultural contributions of immigrants from many traditions, but blessed with one common language that has united a diverse nation and fostered harmony among its people.

As much by accident as by design, that language is English. Given our country's history of immigration and the geography of immigrant settlements, it might have been Dutch, or Spanish, or German; or it might have been two languages, as is the case in Canada, our neighbor to the North.

But English prevailed, and it has served us well. Its eloquence shines in our Declaration of Independence and in our Constitution. It is the living carrier of our democratic ideals.

English is a world language which we share with many other nations. It is the most popular medium of international communication.

*The Spread of Language Segregation*

The United States has been spared the bitter conflicts that plague so many countries whose citizens do not share a common tongue. Historic forces made English the language of all Americans, though nothing in our laws designated it the official language of the nation.

But now English is under attack, and we must take affirmative steps to guarantee that it continues to be our common heritage. Failure to do so may well lead to institutionalized language segregation and a gradual loss of national unity.

The erosion of English and the rise of other languages in public life have several causes:

- Some spokesmen for ethnic groups reject the "melting pot" ideal; they label assimilation a betrayal of their native cultures and demand government funding to maintain separate ethnic institutions.
- Well intentioned but unproven theories have led to extensive government-funded bilingual education programs, ranging from preschool through college.
- New civil rights assertions have yielded bilingual and multilingual ballots, voting instructions, election site counselors, and government-funded voter registration campaigns aimed solely at speakers of foreign languages.
- Record immigration, concentrated in fewer language groups, is reinforcing language segregation and retarding language assimilation.
- The availability of foreign language electronic media, with a full range of news and entertainment, is a new disincentive to the learning of English.

**U.S. ENGLISH:** *A Timely Public Response*

In 1981, Senator S. I. Hayakawa, himself an immigrant and distinguished scholar of semantics, proposed a Constitutional Amendment designating English as the official language of the United States. Senator Hayakawa helped found *U.S. ENGLISH* in 1983 to organize and support a citizens' movement to maintain our common linguistic heritage.

*U.S. ENGLISH* is committed to promoting the use of English in the political, economic, and intellectual life of the nation. It operates squarely within the American political mainstream, and rejects all manifestations of cultural or linguistic chauvinism.

*Our Guiding Principles*

Our goal is to maintain the blessing of a common language—English—for the people of the United States.

These principles guide us:

- In a pluralistic nation such as ours, government should foster the similarities that unite us rather than the differences that separate us.
- The nation's public schools have a special responsibility to help students who don't speak English to learn the language as quickly as possible.
- Quality teaching of English should be part of every student's curriculum, at every academic level.
- The study of foreign languages should be strongly encouraged, both as an academic discipline and for practical, economic, and foreign policy considerations.
- *All* candidates for U.S. citizenship should be required to demonstrate the ability to understand, speak, read and write simple English, and demonstrate basic understanding of our system of government.
- The rights of individuals and groups to use other languages and to establish *privately funded* institutions for the maintenance of diverse languages and cultures must be understood and respected in a pluralistic society.

*Our Action Program*

*U.S. ENGLISH* actively works to reverse the spread to foreign language usage in the nation's official life. Our program calls for:

- Adoption of a Constitutional Amendment to establish English as the official language of the United States.
- Repeal of laws mandating multilingual ballots and voting materials.
- Restriction of government funding for bilingual education to short-term transitional programs only.
- Universal enforcement of the English language and civics requirement for naturalization.

Towards these ends *U.S. ENGLISH* serves as a national center for consultation and cooperation on ways to defend English as the sole official language of the United States. It directs its efforts to leading a public discussion on the best language polices for our multi-ethnic society; educating opinion leaders on the long-term implications of language segregation; securing more balanced treatment of the issue in the media; and encouraging research on improved methods of teaching English.

*We Need Your Help*

*U.S. ENGLISH* welcomes to membership all people who are concerned about the prospect of entrenched language segregation and the possibility of losing our strongest national bond.

We hope that you will join us and defend our common language against misguided policies that threaten our national unity.

private sector, the profit motive promotes multilingual accommodation in businesses, and in many communities advertising and marketing in several languages is the norm. Several major metropolitan areas, for example, support classified telephone directories in languages other than English. Nevertheless, English-only legislation opens the door to restrictions on public service assistance and free speech.

A friend of mine, a physician, voted in favor of an amendment to the California Constitution declaring English as the official language. He explained, "People come into my office every day, and they can't speak a word of English." His reasoning is flawed, because people cannot be legislated into English proficiency. Proposed legislation ignores the need for wide-scale programs to assist newcomers in learning English. It would be far more useful to expand underfunded adult education programs, where waiting lists for English classes are common. In general, limitations on language use threaten to exclude large sectors of our population from the mainstream instead of providing the education and services necessary to enfranchise them.

In *Meyer v. Nebraska,* the Supreme Court was succinct and eloquent:

The protection of the Constitution extends to all—to those who speak other languages as well as to those born with English on the tongue. Perhaps it would be highly advantageous if all had ready understanding of our ordinary speech, but this cannot be coerced by methods which conflict with the Constitution—a desirable end cannot be promoted by prohibited means.

## NATIONAL UNITY AND DIVERSITY

Our national motto is *"E Pluribus Unum"*—one out of many. Much of our political heritage has evolved from the tension implicit in the complex philosophy underlying those three words. While we hope to forge one nation from our many peoples and cultures, the nation we intend to create is one that protects our individual right to maintain our differences. As the nation progresses and grows, we try to make sense out of U.S. society. It is difficult to decide who we are, since U.S. identity is complex and constantly changing. Social scientists have analyzed trends in our thinking about Americanization.

### Assimilationism versus Pluralism

In the eighteenth and nineteenth centuries, political emphasis was placed on the concept of *unum,* which was crystallized at the beginning of the twentieth century into the image of the "melting pot" (Gleason, 1984). While the melting pot was envisioned as a process of ethnic and racial fusion, it can also be seen as a call for Anglo-conformity. In the melting pot, a person was expected to Americanize—to emerge looking, sounding, and acting like a white person of northern European background. *Melting* was a misnomer in this context, because it did not involve a synthesis of all the elements involved.

As the various ethnic groups comprising the population of the United States have established themselves socially and politically, they have begun to view their ethnic heritages from a positive perspective. Emphasis has moved to *pluribus;* a cultural pluralist view of American society has emerged, suggesting that it is possible to be unified while still maintaining diversity. The most common analogy for the cultural pluralist view is the salad bowl. All the ingredients in a salad make contributions to the whole, but each one maintains its own distinguishable identity. Strict adherence, however, to the dichotomy between assimilationist and pluralist philosophies is misleading and oversimplified.

Only about 14 percent of the population has Anglo-Saxon heritage, and we are increasingly a nation of minorities. North American ethnicities have persisted with a wide range of manifestations. American Amish, for example, live in separate enclaves, maintaining their own distinctive social organization and language. At the other end of the spectrum, many Americans function almost exclusively in the mainstream, affirming their ethnicity only on special occasions, with traditional food, dress, and rituals. In other words, ethnicity itself has been altered by the American experience, and to that extent we can lay claim to an assimilationist tradition.

Lambert and Taylor (1987) surveyed members of ethnolinguistic minorities in Detroit and found that families who have been here several generations and newly arrived immigrants alike affirm the importance of maintaining cultural heritage and heritage languages. The researchers' comments on their findings sum up the paradox of American identity:

The irony in all this is that in striving to preserve ethnic heritages while escaping Americanization, immigrant groups may be contributing more to what America seems now to be than they might realize. They can, it seems, be themselves and in so doing be as American as anyone else. This, of course, would make the process of not becoming too American much easier for them because, in one sense *not being* American gets progressively closer to *being* American. (p. 70)

## American Identity and Language

The language situation in the United States, as we have discussed in preceding chapters, is extremely complex. English clearly dominates as our national language, but in addition we have within our borders a vast array of indigenous and immigrant languages. While there are unquestionably large numbers of people whose first language is not English, there are also many who maintain vestiges of ethnic heritage languages for symbolic purposes rather than day-to-day communication.

From a legal perspective, U.S. language policies reside in a variety of federal and state statutes and cases, thus becoming thoroughly inconsistent. Piatt (1986) illustrates the inconsistencies with the hypothetical case of Ms. Martinez, who is Spanish-speaking and whose English is limited. Ms. Martinez's troubles occur in a hypothetical jurisdiction, but Piatt's analysis of language policy is based on real law. And while the example is framed in terms of a Spanish speaker, the policies apply to speakers of any language other than English.

In the course of one wearisome day, Ms. Martinez discovers that she can be fired from her job for speaking Spanish to co-workers in front of customers, but she cannot be ejected from a bar for speaking Spanish to fellow beer drinkers. She owes money to two department stores, and both of them are suing her. Her lack of English makes it difficult for her to understand either summons. She throws one away, resulting in a default judgment against her, and answers the second as best she can. How could Ms. Martinez have guessed that it would have been better to toss both summonses in the wastebasket? Courts have set aside default judgments resulting from language barriers, but Ms. Martinez may not be entitled to an interpreter if she tries to defend herself in the second case. Her children are doing poorly in school due to lack of English proficiency. Ms. Martinez can demand comprehensible instruction for her Spanish-speaking children, but she cannot demand social service assistance in Spanish to keep a roof over her head.

Proponents of English-only policies are threatened by our multilingualism and insist that language diversity should be discouraged since it leads to national disunity. Analysis of language situations around the world disproves that assertion, indicating that linguistic tolerance is far less likely than linguistic repression to lead to disunity. Rather than imposing an oppressive English-only law, we might do well to consider Piatt's (1986) recommendations that we:

- establish a policy of official multilingualism to protect access to legal rights and fulfillment of human needs. This policy would provide services in languages other than English for court proceedings, administrative hearings, hospitals, and so on.
- require use of English where circumstances require a common majority language, for example, in communications between pilots and air traffic control towers
- allow freedom of choice in all other areas

## The Role of the Schools

As discussed in this chapter, schools can be instrumental in supporting minority languages. Bilingual education, however, as it has developed in legislation and implementation, is overwhelmingly transitional in nature. The tendency in the great majority of bilingual programs is not to foster bilingualism. To the contrary, publicly funded programs for limited English proficient children emphasize proficiency in English.

Dual language instruction will persist in a compensatory and transitional mode until the American public begins to understand what privileged classes around the world have always known—that bilingualism is socially, politically, and economically desirable. In discussing American language policy, the sociolinguist Joshua A. Fishman (1981) observed:

> Language policy involves a vision of America. A multilingual enrichment policy envisages a multilingual America as being in the public good. We support a multiparty system. . . . Our anti-trust laws aim to diversify the economic market place. We can similarly diversify the cultural market place. . . . There is a vision of American magnanimity involved, but more than that, a vision of American possibilities, opportunities, appreciations, sensitivities, that we all should savour. (pp. 525–526)

## SUMMARY

Governments have language policies, or ways of promoting the use of particular languages for particular purposes. Governments can promote languages through standardization and dissemination or suppress them by prohibiting their use in the media, public life, and the schools.

In the United States we tend to be linguistically unsophisticated, and our parochial attitudes about multilingualism have hurt us in international trade, national security, and diplomacy. The narrow view we often have about multilingualism, combined with reactions to increased immigration and population changes, provides a growth medium for language restrictionists. Language restrictionism is not new in the United States. The current movement, like its predecessors, is attempting to limit the use of languages other than English in a variety of areas.

It is difficult to characterize American identity. While assimilationism and pluralism seem to represent polar opposites, in fact Americanization is a process that includes both. National language policy is unclear, but multiple languages are part of our American identity and are also socially, politically, and economically valuable. Schools can assist in promoting positive bilingualism for all children, but that will require rethinking our national position on dual language instruction.

## ACTIVITIES AND QUESTIONS TO THINK ABOUT

1. Survey colleagues or classmates who have been educated outside the United States. Find out what the requirements were for foreign language learning in their native schools.
2. Survey high schools and colleges in your area. What, if any, are the foreign language requirements for graduation? What languages are offered? Which ones have the highest enrollments?
3. Survey friends, relatives, and colleagues. Ask how many of them would like to know another language. How many would favor foreign or modern language instruction in the schools? How many of them consider bilingual education desirable for limited English proficient children?
4. Is there a local ordinance, a statewide law, or language in the state constitution amendment that makes English the official language in your area? Is such legislation under consideration? What are the potential impacts of such legislation?
5. Create an ethnic profile of the students in your class. How many different backgrounds are represented? To what extent do those having foreign backgrounds feel they have maintained ties with their ethnic heritage(s)? With their language(s)? How do they feel about their relationship to their ethnic and linguistic heritage(s)?

## SUGGESTIONS FOR FURTHER READING

Adams, K. L., and Brink, D. T. (1990). *Perspectives on official English: The campaign for English as the official language of the USA.* Berlin: Mouton de Gruyter.
This book contains an overview of the general issue of language policy and analyses of language policy around the world. The book then zeroes in on language policy in the United States with a detailed discussion of California's English only proposition, as well as discussions of language use and legislation in Florida, New York, and parts of the Southwest. One whole section is devoted to language legislation from the perspective of constitutional law. An appendix contains language legislation from several states, as of 1990.
Baron, D. (1990). *The English-only question: An official language for Americans?* New Haven: Yale University Press.
This book is a detailed history of language policy in the United States. An appendix contains a map overviewing state legislation on English-only as of mid-1990.

Crawford, J. (1992a). *Hold your tongue: Bilingualism and the politics of "English Only."* Reading, MA: Addison-Wesley.
This book is a readable and comprehensive analysis of the English-only movement in the United States.

Crawford, J. (Ed.). (1992b). *Language loyalties: A source book on the official English controversy.* Chicago: The University of Chicago Press.
A collection of articles and legal documents that reflect on language issues in every area of public life, this is an invaluable collection for a serious student of American language policy.

Eastman, C. M. (1983). *Language planning: An introduction.* San Francisco: Chandler & Sharp.
Information on language planning, a relatively new branch of sociolinguistics, is primarily available in articles and books written for professionals in the field. This book provides an introduction from an interdisciplinary perspective, relating language issues to economics, politics, and social sciences. An appendix by Thomas Reese and Jonathan Pool provides a list of resources on language planning.

Edwards, J. (Ed.). (1984). *Linguistic minorities, policies and pluralism.* London: Academic Press.
Articles in this book analyze language policy with reference to language minorities in Finland, Great Britain, Canada, Australia, and the United States. Several articles deal with the social and political implications of multilingualism and cultural pluralism. Philip Gleason's article is a detailed history of the concepts of pluralism and assimilation as they have developed in the United States.

Ferguson, C. A., & Heath, S. B. (1981). *Language in the USA.* New York: Cambridge University Press.
A collection of articles on describing and analyzing language in the United States, including American English, languages before English, and languages that continue to exist despite the dominance of English. Social and political aspects of language planning and the history and future of U.S. language policy are considered.

Haugen, E. (1987). *Blessings of Babel: Bilingualism and language planning.* Berlin: Mouton de Gruyter.
Not intended for the layperson or the beginner, this discussion of bilingualism in individuals and societies is nevertheless recommended as a synthesis of up-to-date thinking in the area of sociolinguistics. The author's personal observations as a bilingual person add a note of warmth and familiarity to abstract concepts of language contact, language shift, and language planning.

Kloss, H. (1977). *The American bilingual tradition.* Rowley, MA: Newbury House.
Already recommended in Chapter 1, this book bears another mention as a classic analysis of U.S. language policy.

Liebowitz, A. H. (1971). *Educational policy and political acceptance: The imposition of English as the language of instruction in American schools.* Washington, DC: Center for Applied Linguistics. (ERIC Document Reproduction Service No. ED 047 321).
Current discussion of language restrictionism relies heavily on this and other works by Arnold Liebowitz on the history of U.S. language policy. This study analyzes the experience of German Americans, Mexican Americans, Japanese Americans, American Indians, and Puerto Ricans in public schools.

Piatt, B. (1990). *¿Only English? Law and language policy in the United States.* Albuquerque: University of New Mexico Press.

A historical and legal analysis of American language policy, this book calls for a balanced formulation of language policy that can meet our political and personal needs in a multicultural and multilingual society.

Simon, P. (1980). *The tongue-tied American*. New York: Continuum.
A collection of data, anecdotes, and information that illustrates the sorry state of foreign language learning in the United States, this book highlights the outcomes of our national monolingualism in the areas of international trade, national security, and diplomacy. A discussion of language education in elementary, secondary, and post-secondary education is included, as well as explanation of several methods of second language instruction.

Spolsky, B. (Ed.). (1986). *Language and education in multilingual settings*. San Diego, CA: College-Hill Press.
The articles contained in this book address language policy and planning issues from the perspective of the need to provide first language instruction for language minority children, and the problems inherent in developing instructional models that are appropriate for them. Several articles address bilingualism and education in the former Soviet Union, Ireland, New Zealand, Namibia, and the Philippines. Other articles analyze theoretical perspectives using examples from around the world.

Van Horne, W. A., & Tonnesen, T. V. (1987). *Ethnicity and language*. Milwaukee: The University of Wisconsin System Institute on Race and Ethnicity.
One of a series of six volumes on ethnicity and public policy published by the University of Wisconsin System, this book contains articles about language policy, bilingual education, foreign language study, and the needs of children from different ethnic backgrounds in the United States.

Wolfson, N., & Manes, J. (Eds.). (1985). *Language of inequality*. Berlin: Mouton.
A collection of articles designed to provide an overview of the sociolinguistics of language contact, this book includes discussions of language maintenance, language shift, and language policy and planning around the world.

# Bibliography

Adams, K. L., & Brink, D. T. (Eds.). (1990). *Perspectives on official English: The campaign for English as the official language of the USA.* Berlin: Mouton de Gruyter.

Ambert, A. N., & Melendez, S. E. (1985). *Bilingual education: A sourcebook.* New York: Teachers College Press.

American Speech-Language-Hearing Association. (1983). *Committee on Language Report,* ASHA, 25(6).

Amoriggi, H. D., & Gefteas, D. J. (1981). *Affective considerations in bilingual education: Problems and solutions.* Rosslyn, VA: National Clearinghouse for Bilingual Education.

Arons, S. (1983). *Compelling belief: The culture of American schooling.* New York: McGraw-Hill.

Arvizu, S. F., Snyder, W. A., & Espinosa, P. T. (1980). *Demystifying the concept of culture: Theoretical and conceptual tools.* Los Angeles: Evaluation, Dissemination and Assessment Center, California State University, Los Angeles.

Asher, J. J. (1982). The total physical response approach. In R. W. Blair (Ed.), *Innovative approaches to language learning* (pp. 54–66). Rowley, MA: Newbury House.

Asher, J. J. (1986). *Learning another language through actions: The complete teacher's guidebook.* Los Gatos, CA: Sky Oaks Productions.

*Aspira of New York v. Board of Education of the City of New York,* Civ. No. 4002 (S.D. N.Y. consent agreement, August 29, 1974).

Au, K. H., & Jordan, C. (1981). Teaching reading to Hawaiian children: Finding a culturally appropriate solution. In H. T. Trueba, C. P. Guthrie, & K. H. Au (Eds.), *Culture and the bilingual classroom: Studies in classroom ethnography* (pp. 139–152). Rowley, MA: Newbury House.

Baker, K. A., & de Kanter, A. A. (1981, September 25). *Effectiveness of bilingual education: A review of the literature.* Washington, DC: Office of Planning, Budget and Evaluation, U.S. Department of Education.

Bancroft, W. J. (1978). The Lozanov method and its American adaptations. *Modern Language Journal, 62,* 167–174.

Banks, J. A. (1977). *Multiethnic education: Practices and promises.* Bloomington, IN: Phi Delta Kappa Educational Foundation.

Baron, D. (1990). *The English-only question: An official language for Americans?* New Haven: Yale University Press.

Battle in Spain on teaching in Spanish. (1993, November). *New York Times,* p. A4.

Beardsley, T. (1995, January). For whom the bell curve really tolls. *Scientific American, 272*(1), pp. 14, 16–17.

Bell, L. A. (1991). Changing our ideas about ourselves: Group consciousness raising with elementary school girls as a means to empowerment. In C. E. Sleeter (Ed.), *Empowerment through multicultural education* (pp. 229–249). Albany: State University of New York Press.

Benderson, A. (1983). *Foreign languages in the schools.* Princeton, NJ: Educational Testing Service (ERIC Document Reproduction Service No. ED 239 516).

Bereiter, C., & Engelmann, S. (1966). *Teaching disadvantaged children in the pre-school.* Englewood Cliffs, NJ: Prentice-Hall.

Bialystok, E. (Ed.) (1991). *Language processing in bilingual children.* Cambridge, Eng.: Cambridge University Press.

Bilingual Education Act, as amended, 20 U.S.C. sec. 3221 et seq.

Bilingual programs in Sweden are truly so. (1985). *The Reading Teacher, 39,* 213.

Blair, R. W. (Ed.). (1982). *Innovative approaches to language teaching.* Rowley, MA: Newbury House.

Bloom, L., & Lahey, M. (1978). *Language development and language disorders.* New York: John Wiley & Sons.

Bloomfield, L. (1933). *Language.* New York: Holt, Rinehart, and Winston.

Boykin, A. W. (1984). Reading achievement and the social-cultural frame of reference of Afro-American children. *Journal of Negro Education, 53,* 464–473.

Brown, H. D. (1980). *Principles of language learning and teaching.* Englewood Cliffs, NJ: Prentice-Hall.

Brown, H. D. (1987). *Principles of language learning and teaching* (2nd ed.). Englewood Cliffs, NJ: Prentice-Hall.

Brown, J. E. (Ed.). (1972). *The North American Indians: A selection of photographs by Edward S. Curtis.* Millerton, NY: Aperture.

Brown, R., Cazden, C., & Bellugi, U. (1973). The child's grammar from I to III. In C. Ferguson and D. Slobin (Eds.), *Studies of child language development* (pp. 295–333). New York: Holt, Rinehart, & Winston.

*Brown v. Board of Education of Topeka,* 347 U.S. 483 (1954).

Bryson, B. (1994). *Made in America: An informal history of the English language in the United States.* New York: William Morrow.

Butterfield, F. (1986, August 3). Why Asians are going to the head of the class. *The New York Times,* Sec. XII, pp. 18–19.

Butterfield, F. (1994, December 30). Programs seek to stop trouble before it starts. *The New York Times,* p. A11.

Cage, M. C. (1994, October 12). Spanish, Si! *The Chronicle of Higher Education,* pp. A15, A17.

California State Department of Education (Ed.). (1986). *Beyond language: Social and cultural factors in schooling language minority students.* Los Angeles: Evaluation, Dissemina-tion and Assessment Center, California State University, Los Angeles.

California State Department of Education (Ed.). (1994). *Schooling and language minority students: A theoretical framework* (2nd ed.). Sacramento, CA: Bilingual Education Office.

California State Department of Education (1984). *Studies on immersion education: A collection for United States educators.* Sacramento, CA: Office of Bilingual Bicultural Education.

Campbell-Jones, S. (Producer). (1985). *Baby talk* [video]. San Diego: Media Guild.

Canale, M., & Swain, M. (1980). Theoretical bases of communicative approaches to second language teaching and testing. *Applied Linguistics, 1,* 1-47.

Carter, T. P. (1970). *Mexican Americans in school: A history of educational neglect.* New York: College Entrance Examination Board.

*Castañeda v. Pickard,* 648 F.2d 989 (5th Cir. 1981).

Castellanos, D. (1983). *The best of two worlds: Bilingual bicultural education in the U.S.* Trenton, NJ: New Jersey State Department of Education.

Chaika, E. (1989). *Language: The social mirror* (2nd ed.). Rowley, MA: Newbury House.

Chamot, A. U., & O'Malley, J. M. (1987). The cognitive academic language learning approach: A bridge to the mainstream. *TESOL Quarterly, 21,* 227-249.

Chamot, A. U., & O'Malley, J. M. (1994). *The CALLA handbook: Implementing the cognitive academic language learning approach.* New York: Addison-Wesley.

Chavez, L. (1987, January 29). Struggling to keep Spanish in U.S. pure. *The New York Times,* Section II, p. 1.

Cheng, L. L. (1987). *Assessing Asian language performance: Guidelines for evaluating limited-English-proficient students.* Rockville, MD: Aspen Publishers.

Civil Rights Act of 1964, 42 U.S.C. sec. 2000(d).

Cohen, A. D. (1980). *Testing language ability in the classroom.* Rowley, MA: Newbury House.

Cohen, E. G. (1986). *Designing groupwork: Strategies for the heterogeneous classroom.* New York: Teachers College Press.

Collier, V. P. (1987). The effect of age on acquisition of a second language for school. *New Focus, 1*(2).

Contín, M. (1995, February 1). U. S. Ninth Circuit Court reverses Arizona English-only. *NABE News,* p. 1.

Cortés, C. E. (1986). The education of language minority students: A contextual interaction model. In California State Department of Education (Ed.), *Beyond language: Social and cultural factors in schooling language minority students* (pp. 3-33). Los Angeles: Evaluation, Dissemination and Assessment Center, California State University, Los Angeles.

Cortés, C. E. (March/April, 1990). Multicultural education: A curricular basic for our multiethnic future. *Doubts and Certainties, 4*(78), 1-5.

Crawford, J. (1986, April 23). Immersion method is faring poorly in bilingual study. *Education Week,* pp. 1, 10.

Crawford, J. (1989). *Bilingual education: History, politics, theory, and practice.* Trenton, NJ: Crane.

Crawford, J. (1992a). *Hold your tongue: Bilingualism and the politics of "English only."* Reading, MA: Addison-Wesley.

Crawford, J. (1992b). *Language loyalties: A source book on the official English controversy.* Chicago: University of Chicago Press.

Crystal, D. (1987). *The Cambridge encyclopedia of language.* Cambridge, Eng.: Cambridge University Press.

Cummins, J. (1981). The role of primary language development in promoting educational success for language minority students. In California State Department of Education (Ed.), *Schooling and language minority students: A theoretical framework* (pp. 3-49). Los Angeles: Evaluation, Dissemination and Assessment Center, California State University, Los Angeles.

Cummins, J. (1984a). *Bilingualism and special education: Issues in assessment and pedagogy.* San Diego, CA: College-Hill Press.

Cummins, J. (1984b). Linguistic minorities and multicultural policy in Canada. In J. Edwards (Ed.), *Linguistic minorities, policies and pluralism* (pp. 81–105). London: Academic Press.

Cummins, J. (1989). *Empowering minority students.* Sacramento, CA: California Association of Bilingual Education.

Cummins, J. (1994). Primary language instruction and the education of language minority students. In California State Department of Education (Ed.), *Schooling and language minority students: A theoretical framework* (2nd ed.) (pp. 3–46). Los Angeles: Evaluation, Dissemination and Assessment Center, California State University, Los Angeles.

Cummins, J., & Swain, M. (1986). *Bilingualism in education.* White Plains, NY: Longman.

Curran, C. A. (1982). Community language learning. In R. W. Blair (Ed.), *Innovative approaches to language teaching* (pp. 118–133). Rowley, MA: Newbury House.

Danoff, M. N., Coles, G. J., McLaughlin, D. H., & Reynolds, D. J. (1977a). *Evaluation of the impact of ESEA Title VII Spanish/English bilingual education programs, Volume I: Study design and interim findings.* Palo Alto, CA: American Institutes for Research.

Danoff, M. N., Coles, G. J., McLaughlin, D. H., & Reynolds, D. J. (1977b). *Evaluation of the impact of ESEA Title VII Spanish/English bilingual education programs, Volume II: Project descriptions.* Palo Alto, CA: American Institutes for Research.

Danoff, M. N., Coles, G. J., McLaughlin, D. H., & Reynolds, D. J. (1978). *Evaluation of the impact of ESEA Title VII Spanish/English bilingual education programs, Volume III: Year two impact data, educational process, and in-depth analysis.* Palo Alto, CA: American Institutes for Research.

Day, E. C. (1981). Assessing communicative competence: Integrative testing of second language learners. In J. U. Erickson & D. R. Omark (Eds.), *Communication assessment of the bilingual bicultural child: Issues and guidelines* (pp. 179–197). Baltimore: University Park Press.

Day, E. C., McCollum, P. A., Cieslak, V. A., & Erickson, J. G. (1981). Discrete point language tests of bilinguals: A review of selected tests. In J. G. Erickson & D. R. Omark (Eds.), *Communication assessment of the bilingual bicultural child: Issues and guidelines* (pp. 129–161). Baltimore: University Park Press.

DeAvila, E., Duncan, S., & Navarrete, C. (1987). *Finding Out/Descubrimiento.* Northvale, NJ: Santillana.

de Villiers, P. A., & de Villiers, J. G. (1979). *Early language.* Cambridge, MA: Harvard University Press.

Diller, K. C. (1978). *The language teaching controversy.* Rowley, MA: Newbury House.

Doerner, W. R. (1987, September 14). Troubles of a tongue en crise. *Newsweek,* p. 49.

Eastman, C. M. (1983). *Language planning: An introduction.* San Francisco: Chandler & Sharp.

Edwards, J. (Ed.). (1984). *Linguistic minorities, policies and pluralism.* London: Academic Press.

Elford, G., & Woodford, P. (1982). *A study of bilingual instructional practices in nonpublic schools: Final report.* Princeton, NJ: Educational Testing Service. (ERIC Document Reproduction Service No. ED 240 855).

Ellis, R. (1988). Theories of second language acquisition. In P. A. Richard-Amato (Ed.), *Making it happen: Interaction in the second language classroom, from theory to practice* (pp. 319–329). White Plains, NY: Longman.

Equal Educational Opportunities Act of 1974, 20 U.S.C. 1703(f).

Erickson, J. G., & Omark, D. R. (Eds.). (1981). *Communication assessment of the bilingual bicultural child: Issues and guidelines.* Baltimore: University Park Press.

Ervin-Tripp, S. M. (1976). Language development. *Psychological Documents, 6, 4.* (Ms. No. 1336).

Escamilla, K. (1980). German-English bilingual schools 1870–1917: Cultural and linguistic survival in St. Louis. *Bilingual Journal, 5*(2), 16–20.

Escamilla, K. (1993). Promoting biliteracy: Issues in promoting English literacy in students acquiring English. In J. V. Tinajero and A. Flor Ada (Eds.), *The power of two languages* (pp. 220–233). New York: Macmillan/McGraw-Hill.

Ferguson, C. A. (1978). Language and global interdependence. In E. M. Gerli, J. E. Alatis, & R. I. Brod (Eds.), *Language in American life: Proceedings of the Georgetown University Modern Language Association Conference October 6–8, 1977, Washington, DC* (pp. 23–31). Washington, DC: Georgetown University Press.

Ferguson, C. A., & Heath, S. B. (Eds.). (1981). *Language in the USA.* New York: Cambridge University Press.

Feuerstein, R. (1978). *The dynamic assessment of retarded performers: The learning potential assessment device, theory, instruments, and techniques.* Baltimore, MD: University Park Press.

Fincher, B. H. (1978). Bilingualism in contemporary China: The coexistence of oral diversity and written uniformity. In B. Spolsky and R. L. Cooper (Eds.), *Case studies in bilingual education* (pp. 72–87). Rowley, MA: Newbury House.

Fishman, J. (1985). *Ethnicity in action: The community resources of ethnic languages in the United States.* Binghamton, NY: Bilingual Press/Editorial Bilingüe.

Fishman, J. A. (1981). Language policy: Past, present and future. In C. A. Ferguson & S. B. Heath (Eds.), *Language in the USA* (pp. 516–526). New York: Cambridge University Press.

Fishman, J. A., Gertner, M. H., Lowy, E. G., & Milan, W. G. (Eds.). (1985). *The rise and fall of the ethnic revival: Perspectives on language and ethnicity.* Berlin: Mouton.

Fishman, J. A., & Keller, G. D. (Eds.). (1982). *Bilingual education for Hispanic students in the United States.* New York: Teachers College Press.

Flor Ada, A. (1988). The Pajaro Valley experience: Working with Spanish-speaking parents to develop children's reading and writing skills through the use of children's literature. In T. Skutnabb-Kangas & J. Cummins (Eds.) *Minority Education: From Shame to Struggle.* Clevedon, Eng.: Multilingual Matters.

Foley, D. E. (1994). Reconsidering anthropological explanations of minority school failure. In F. Schultz (Ed.), *Multicultural Education 94/95.* Guildford, CT: Dushkin.

Fordham, S. (1991). Peer-proofing academic competition among black adolescents: "Acting White" black American style. In C. E. Sleeter (Ed.) *Empowerment through multicultural education* (pp. 69–93). Albany: State University of New York Press.

Freeman, D. E., & Freeman, Y. S. (1994). *Between worlds: Access to second language acquisition.* Portsmouth, NH: Heinemann.

Freire, P. (1970). *Pedagogy of the oppressed.* New York: The Seabury Press.

Garcia, E., & Figueroa, R. A. (Fall, 1994). Issues in testing students from culturally and linguistically diverse backgrounds. *Multicultural Education, 2*(1), 10–19.

Garnica, O. K. (1977). Some prosodic and paralinguistic features of speech to young children. In C. E. Snow & C. A. Ferguson (Eds.), *Talking to children* (pp. 63–88). New York: Cambridge University Press.

Genesee, F. (1987). *Learning through two languages: Studies of immersion and bilingual education.* Cambridge, MA: Newbury House.

Genesee, F. (Ed.) (1994). *Educating second language children: The whole child, the whole curriculum, the whole community.* Cambridge, Eng.: Cambridge University Press.

Genesee, F., & Hamayan, E. V. (1994). Classroom-based assessment. In F. Genesee (Ed.) *Educating second language children: The whole child, the whole curriculum, the whole community.* Cambridge, Eng.: Cambridge University Press.

Giroux, H. (1988, March). *Teacher empowerment and the struggle for public life.* Paper presented at San Jose State University, San Jose, CA.

Givón, T. (1985). Function, structure, and language acquisition. In D. I. Slobin (Ed.), *The crosslinguistic study of language acquisition: Vol. 2. Theoretical issues* (pp. 1005–1027). Hillsdale, NJ: Lawrence Erlbaum.

Gleason, J. B. (1973). Code switching in children's language. In T. E. Moore (Ed.), *Cognitive development and the acquisition of language* (pp. 159–167). New York: Academic Press.

Gleason, J. B. (1985). Studying language development. In J. B. Gleason (Ed.), *The development of language* (pp. 1–35). Columbus, OH: Merrill.

Gleason, P. (1984). Pluralism and assimilation: A conceptual history. In J. Edwards (Ed.), *Linguistic minorities, policies and pluralism* (pp. 221–257). London: Academic Press.

Goldhor Lerner, H. (September, 1993). Good advice. *New Woman,* p. 40.

*Gomez v. Illinois State Board of Education,* 811 F.2d 1030 (7th Cir. 1987).

Gonzalez, A., & Guerrero, M. (1983). *A cooperative/interdependent approach to bilingual education.* Hollister, CA: Hollister School District.

Gonzalez, G., & Maez, L. F. (1980). To switch or not to switch: The role of code-switching in the elementary bilingual classroom. In R. V. Padilla (Ed.), *Ethnoperspectives in bilingual education research: Theory in bilingual education* (pp. 125–135). Ypsilanti, MI: Eastern Michigan University.

Goodenough, W. (1971). *Culture, language, and society.* Reading, MA: Addison-Wesley.

Graves, B., & Rubenstein, S. (1995, January 20). Setting the standard: Oregon adopts new requirements for school graduation. *The Oregonian,* pp. B1, B4.

Gray, P. (Fall, 1993). Teach your children well [Special Issue]. *Time,* pp. 69–71.

Grittner, F. M. (1969). *Teaching foreign languages.* New York: Harper & Row.

Grosjean, F. (1982). *Life with two languages.* Cambridge, MA: Harvard University Press.

Growth of a nation. (1985, July 8). *Newsweek,* pp. 34–35.

Guido, M. (1995, March 16). Model escuela: Two-way language immersion program to be emulated by schools in other regions. *San Jose Mercury News,* pp. 1A, 22A.

Gumperz, J. J. (1981). Conversational inference and classroom learning. In J. L. Green & C. Wallat (Eds.), *Ethnography and language in educational settings* (pp. 3–23). Norwood, NJ: Ablex.

Hakuta, K. (1985, December). Bilingualism and its potential impact on the nation's schools. *CABE Newsletter,* pp. 1, 5, 13.

Hakuta, K. (1986). *Mirror of language: The debate on bilingualism.* New York: Basic Books.

Hakuta, K., & Gould, L. J. (1987). Synthesis of research on bilingual education. *Educational Leadership, 44*(6), 38–45.

Hall, E. T. (1959). *The silent language.* Garden City, NY: Doubleday.

Hall, E. T. (1966). *The hidden dimension.* Garden City, NY: Doubleday.

Hamayan, E. (1990). Preparing mainstream teachers for teaching potentially English proficient students. In Office of Bilingual Education & Minority Language Affairs (Ed.), *Proceedings of the first research symposium on limited English proficient students' issues* (pp. 1–22). Washington, DC: U.S. Department of Education.

Hamayan, E. V., & Perlman, R. (1990, Spring). *Helping language minority students after they exit from bilingual/ESL programs: A handbook for teachers.* Rosslyn, VA: National Clearinghouse for Bilingual Education.

Harman, S. (1991). One more critique of testing—with two differences. In Edelsky, C. (Ed.), *With literacy and justice for all: Rethinking the social in language and education.* London: The Falmer Press.

Haugen, E. (1987). *Blessings of Babel: Bilingualism and language planning.* Berlin: Mouton de Gruyter.

Hayes, C. W., Ornstein, J., & Gage, W. W. (1977). *ABC's of language and linguistics: A practical primer to language science in today's world.* Silver Spring, MD: Institute of Modern Languages.

Heath, S. B. (1983). Language policies. *Society, 20*(4), 57–63.

Here they come, ready or not. (1986, May 14). *Education Week,* pp. 14–39.

Hernandez-Chavez, E., Burt, M., & Dulay, H. (1978). Language dominance and proficiency testing: Some general considerations. *NABE Journal, 3*(1), 41–54.

Howard, D. P. (1982). Pitfalls in the multicultural diagnostic/remedial process: A Central American experience. *Journal of Multilingual and Multicultural Development, 3,* pp. 41–46.

Hudelson, S. (1994). Literacy development of second language children. In Genesee, F. (Ed.), *Educating second language children: The whole child, the whole curriculum, the whole community* (pp. 129–158). Cambridge, Eng.: Cambridge University Press.

*Idaho Migrant Council v. Board of Education,* 647 F.2d 69 (9th Cir. 1981).

Igoa, Cristina. (1995). *The inner world of the immigrant child.* New York: St. Martin's Press.

Immigration Project of the National Lawyers Guild, The (1981). *Immigration law and defense* (2nd ed.). New York: Clark Boardman.

Jacobson, R. (April, 1987). *Allocating two languages as a key feature of a bilingual methodology.* Paper presented at the meeting of the National Association for Bilingual Education, Denver, CO.

Jensen, A. R. (1969). How much can we boost IQ and scholastic achievement? *Harvard Educational Review, 39,* 1–123.

Kagan, S. (1986). Cooperative learning and sociocultural factors in schooling. In California State Department of Education (Ed.), *Beyond language: Social and cultural factors in schooling language minority students* (pp. 231–298). Los Angeles: Evaluation, Dissemination and Assessment Center, California State University, Los Angeles.

Kamin, L. J. (1995, February). Behind the curve. *Scientific American,* pp. 99–103.

Karst, K. L. (1986). Paths to belonging: The Constitution and cultural identity. *North Carolina Law Review, 64,* 303–377.

Keller, G. D., & Van Hooft, K. S. (1982). A chronology of bilingualism and bilingual education in the United States. In J. A. Fishman & G. D. Keller (Eds.) (1982), *Bilingual education for Hispanic students in the United States* (pp. 3–19). New York: Teachers College Press.

*Keyes v. School District No. 1,* Denver, 380 F. Supp. 673 (D. Colo. 1974).

*Keyes v. School District No. 1,* Denver, Colorado, 576 F. Supp. 1503 (D. Colo. 1983).

Kirkland, R. I., Jr. (1988, March 14). Entering a new age of boundless competition. *Fortune,* pp. 40–42, 46, 48.

Kjolseth, R. (1976). Bilingual education programs in the United States: For assimilation or pluralism? In F. Cordasco (Ed.), *Bilingual schooling in the United States: A sourcebook for educational personnel* (pp. 122–140). New York: McGraw-Hill.

Kjolseth, R. (1983). Cultural politics and bilingualism. *Society, 20*(4), 40–48.

Kloss, H. (1977). *The American bilingual tradition.* Rowley, MA: Newbury House.

Kondracke, M. (1979, March 31). The ugly American redux. *The New Republic,* pp. 55–62.

Krashen, S. D. (1981). Bilingual education and second language acquisition theory. In California State Department of Education (Ed.), *Schooling and language minority students: A theoretical framework* (pp. 51–79). Los Angeles: Evaluation, Dissemination and Assessment Center, California State University, Los Angeles.

Krashen, S. D., & Biber, D. (1988). *On course: Bilingual education's success in California.* Sacramento, CA: California Association for Bilingual Education.

Krashen, S. D., & Terrell, T. D. (1983). *The natural approach: Language acquisition in the classroom.* San Francisco: Alemany.

Kubchandani, L. M. (1978). Multilingual education in India. In B. Spolsky & R. L. Cooper (Eds.), *Case studies in bilingual education* (pp. 88–125). Rowley, MA: Newbury House Inc.

Labov, W. (1970). *The study of nonstandard English.* Champaign, IL: National Council of the Teachers of English.

LaFontaine, H., Persky, B., & Golubchick, L. H. (Eds.). (1978). *Bilingual education.* Wayne, NJ: Avery.

Lambert, W. E., & Taylor, D. M. (1987). Language minorities in the United States: Conflicts around assimilation and proposed modes of accommodation. In W. A. Van Horne & T. V. Tonnesen (Eds.), *Ethnicity and language* (pp. 58–89). Milwaukee: The University of Wisconsin System Institute on Race and Ethnicity.

Langer, J. A. (Ed.). (1987). *Language, literacy, and culture: Issues of society and schooling.* Norwood, NJ: Ablex.

Langer, J. A. (1991). Literacy and schooling: A sociocognitive perspective. In Hiebert, E. H. (Ed.), *Literacy for a diverse society: Perspectives, practices, and policies* (pp. 9–27). New York: Teachers College Press.

Larsen-Freeman, D., & Long, M. H. (1991). *An introduction to second language research.* White Plains, NY: Longman.

*Lau v. Nichols,* 414 U.S. 563 (1974).

Legarreta-Marcaida, D. (1981). Effective use of the primary language in the classroom. In California State Department of Education (Ed.), *Schooling and language minority students: A theoretical framework* (pp. 83–116). Los Angeles: Evaluation, Dissemination and Assessment Center, California State University, Los Angeles.

Lenneberg, E. (1967). *Biological foundations of language.* New York: John Wiley & Sons.

Lessow-Hurley, J. (1977). *Como ellos lo ven: Migrant children look at life in Longmont.* Boulder, CO: Western Interstate Commission on Higher Education.

Lewis, E. G. (1976). Bilingualism and bilingual education: The ancient world to the Renaissance. In J. A. Fishman (Ed.), *Bilingual education: An international sociological perspective* (pp. 150–200). Rowley, MA: Newbury House.

Lewis, M. (1972). Parents and children: Sex-role development. *School Review, 80,* 229–240.

Liebowitz, A. H. (1971). *Educational policy and political acceptance: The imposition of English as the language of instruction in American schools.* Washington, DC: Center for Applied Linguistics. (ERIC Document Reproduction Service No. ED 047 321).

Liebowitz, A. H. (1978). Language policy in the United States. In H. LaFontaine, B. Persky, & L. H. Golubehick (Eds.), *Bilingual education* (pp. 3–15). Wayne, NJ: Avery.

Lightbown, P., & Spada N. (1993). *How languages are learned.* Oxford: Oxford University Press.

Long, M. H., & Porter, P. A. (1985). Group work, interlanguage talk, and second language acquisition. *TESOL Quarterly, 18,* 207-227.

Lozanov, G. (1982). Suggestology and Suggestopedia. In R. W. Blair (Ed.), *Innovative approaches to language teaching* (pp. 146-159). Rowley, MA: Newbury House.

Macaulay, R. (1980). *Generally speaking: How children learn language.* Rowley, MA: Newbury House.

Mackey, W. F. (1972). *Bilingual education in a binational school.* Rowley, MA: Newbury House.

Mackey, W. F. (1978). The importation of bilingual education models. In J. E. Alatis (Ed.), *Georgetown University round table on languages and linguistics 1978* (pp. 1-18). Washington, DC: Georgetown University Press.

Marin, C., & Macgregor-Scott, P. (Producers). (1987). *Born in East L.A.* [Film]. Universal City, CA: Universal Pictures.

McCollum, P. A., & Day, E. C. (1981). Quasi-integrative approaches: Discrete point scoring of expressive language samples. In J. G. Erickson & D. R. Omark (Eds.), *Communication assessment of the bilingual bicultural child: Issues and guidelines* (pp. 163-177). Baltimore: University Park Press.

McCrum, R., Cran, W., & MacNeil, R. (1986). *The story of English.* New York: Elizabeth Sifton Books (Viking).

McDermott, R. P., & Gospodinoff, K. (1981). Social contexts for ethnic borders and school failure. In H. T. Trueba, G. P. Guthrie, & K. H. Au (Eds.), *Culture and the bilingual classroom: Studies in classroom ethnography* (pp. 212-230). Rowley, MA: Newbury House.

McFadden, B. J. (1983). Bilingual education and the law. *Journal of Law & Education, 12,* 1-27.

Menendez, R., Musca, T., & Olmos, E. J. (Producers). (1988). *Stand and deliver* [Film]. Burbank, CA: Warner Bros.

Mercer, J., & Lewis, J. F. (1979). *System of multicultural pluralistic assessment.* New York: The Psychological Corporation.

Met, M. (1994). Teaching content through a second language. In Genesee, F. (Ed.), *Educating second language children: The whole child, the whole curriculum, the whole community.* Cambridge, Eng.: Cambridge University Press.

*Meyer v. Nebraska,* 262 U.S. 390 (1923).

Miller, J. (1983). *Many voices: Bilingualism, culture and education.* London: Routledge & Kegan Paul.

Mohatt, G. V., & Erickson, F. (1981). Cultural differences in teaching styles in an Odawa school: A sociolinguistic approach. In H. T. Trueba, G. P. Guthrie, & K. H. Au (Eds.), *Culture and the bilingual classroom: Studies in classroom ethnography* (pp. 105-119). Rowley, MA: Newbury House.

*Morgan v. Kerrigan,* 401 F. Supp. 216 (D. Mass. 1975).

Morris, D. (1977). *Manwatching: A field guide to human behavior.* New York: Harry N. Abrams.

Murry, C., & Herrnstein, R. (1994). *The bell curve: The reshaping of American life by differences in intelligence.* New York: The Free Press.

National Board for Professional Teaching Standards. (1993). National Board Certificates. Washington, DC: Author.

National Defense Education Act, 20 U.S.C. sec. 401 et seq., P.L. 85-864, 72 Stat. 1580.

National Public Radio. (March 7, 1995). *Morning Edition.* Washington, DC.

Nieto, S. (Ed.). (1986). Bilingual education and equity, Special issue. *Interracial Books for Children Bulletin, 17*(3 & 4).

Nieto, S. (1992). Affirming diversity: The sociopolitical context of multicultural education. White Plains, NY: Longman.

Nobel, B. L. (1982). *Linguistics for bilinguals*. Rowley, MA: Newbury House.

Office of Bilingual Bicultural Education, California State Department of Education. (1984). *Studies on immersion education: A collection for United States educators*. Sacramento: California State Department of Education.

Ogbu, J. U. (1978). *Minority education and caste: The American system in cross-cultural perspective*. New York: Academic Press.

Ogbu, J. U. (1992). Understanding cultural diversity and learning. *Educational Researcher, 21*(8), 5–14.

Ogbu, J. U. (1994). Racial stratification and education in the United States: Why inequality persists. *Teachers College Record, 96,* 264–298.

Ogbu, J. U., & Matute-Bianchi, M. E. (1986). Understanding sociocultural factors: Knowledge, identity, and school adjustment. In California State Department of Education (Ed.), *Beyond language: Social and cultural factors in schooling language minority students* (pp. 73–142). Los Angeles: Evaluation, Dissemination and Assessment Center, California State University, Los Angeles.

Okazaki, S. (Director). (1987). *Living on Tokyo time* [Film]. Los Angeles: Skouras Pictures.

Oller, J. W., Jr. (1979). *Language tests at school*. White Plains, NY: Longman.

Olsen, L., et al. (1994). *The unfinished journey: Restructuring schools in a diverse society*. San Francisco: California Tomorrow.

O'Malley, J. M., & Valdez Pierce, L. (1991, November). Portfolio assessment: Using portfolio and alternative assessment with LEP students. *Forum, 15*(1), pp. 1–2.

O'Malley, J. M., & Valdez Pierce, L. (1992, Spring). *Performance and portfolio assessment for language minority students*. Washington, DC: National Clearinghouse for Bilingual Education.

Ovando, C. J., & Collier, V. P. (1985). *Bilingual and ESL classrooms*. New York: McGraw-Hill.

Owens, R. E. (1984). *Language development: An introduction*. Columbus, OH: Merrill.

Peregoy, S. F., & Boyle, O. F. (1993). *Reading, writing, & learning in ESL: A resource book for K-8 teachers*. White Plains, NY: Longman.

Pérez, B., & Torres-Guzmán, M. (1992). *Learning in two worlds: An integrated Spanish/ English biliteracy approach*. White Plains, NY: Longman.

Perez, F. (1988, January/February). '88 language battles building in three states. *California Association for Bilingual Education Newsletter,* p. 8.

Perssons, L. (1993). *Parent handbook: Kokopelli's flute*. (Unpublished classroom materials).

Peters, A. M. (1985). Language segmentation: Operating principles for the perception and analysis of language. In D. I. Slobin (Ed.), *The crosslinguistic study of language acquisition: Vol. 2. Theoretical issues* (pp. 1029–1067). Hillsdale, NJ: Lawrence Erlbaum.

Pfeiffer, J. (1988, January). How not to lose the trade wars by cultural gaffes. *Smithsonian,* pp. 145–146, 148, 150–152, 154–155.

Philips, S. U. (1983). *The invisible culture: Communication in classroom and community on the Warm Springs Indian Reservation*. White Plains, NY: Longman.

Piatt, B. (1986). Toward domestic recognition of a human right to language. *Houston Law Review, 23,* 885–906.

Piatt, B. (1990). *¿Only English? Law and language policy in the United States*. Albuquerque: University of New Mexico Press.

*Plessy v. Ferguson,* 163 U.S. 537 (1896).

Ramírez, A. G. (1985). *Bilingualism through schooling: Cross-cultural education for minority and majority students.* Albany: State University of New York Press.

Ramírez, A. G. (1995). *Creating contexts for second language acquisition: Theory and methods.* White Plains, NY: Longman.

Ramírez, D., Yuen, S. D., & Ramey, D. R. (1991). *Final report: Longitudinal study of English immersion strategy, early-exit and late-exit transitional bilingual education programs for language-minority children.* (Department of Education Contract No. 300-87-0156). San Mateo, CA: Aguirre International.

Ramírez, M., & Castañeda, A. (1974). *Cultural democracy, bicognitive development, and education.* New York: Academic Press.

Reacting to *The bell curve.* (1995, January 11). *Education Week,* pp. 29–32.

Rheingold, J. (1988). *They have a word for it.* Los Angeles: Jeremy P. Tarcher.

Richard-Amato, P. A. (1988). *Making it happen: Interaction in the second language classroom from theory to practice.* White Plains, NY: Longman.

Richard-Amato, P. A., & Snow, M. A. (1992). *The multicultural classroom: Readings for content-area teachers.* White Plains, NY: Longman.

Riding, A. (1992, March 3). One caesar salad, garcon, and please hold the French. *The New York Times,* pp. B1, B3.

Riggs, P. (1991). Whole language in TESOL. *TESOL Quarterly, 25,* 521–542.

Rodriguez, R. (1982). *Hunger of memory: The education of Richard Rodriguez.* Boston: David R. Godine.

Rubin, J. (1972). Bilingual usage in Paraguay. In J. A. Fishman (Ed.), *Readings in the sociology of language* (pp. 512–530). The Hague, Neth.: Mouton.

Sachs, J. (1985). Prelinguistic development. In J. B. Gleason (Ed.), *The development of language* (pp. 37–60). Columbus, OH: Merrill.

Samuda, R. J., & Woods, S. L. (Eds.). (1983). *Perspectives in immigrant and minority education.* Lanham, MD: University Press of America.

Saravia-Shore, M., & Arvizu, S. F. (1992). *Cross-cultural literacy: Ethnographies of communication in multiethnic classrooms.* New York: Garland.

Savignon, S. J. (1983). *Communicative competence: Theory and classroom practice.* Reading, MA: Addison-Wesley.

Saville-Troike, M. (1976). Bilingual children: A resource document. In F. Cordasco (Ed.), *Bilingual schooling in the United States: A sourcebook for educational personnel* (pp. 165–188). New York: McGraw-Hill.

Saville-Troike, M. (1982). *The ethnography of communication: An introduction.* Oxford: Basil Blackwell.

Schieffelin, B. B. (1985). The acquisition of Kaluli. In D. I. Slobin (Ed.), *The cross-linguistic study of language acquisition: Vol. 1. The data* (pp. 525–593). Hillsdale, NJ: Lawrence Erlbaum.

Seliger, H. (1977). Does practice make perfect? A study of interaction patterns and L2 competence. *Language Learning, 27*(2), 263–278.

*Serna v. Portales Municipal Schools,* 499 F.2d 1147 (10th Cir. 1974).

Simon, P. (1980). *The tongue-tied American.* New York: Continuum.

Skirts, G. R. (1977). *BáFá BáFá: A cross culture simulation.* Del Mar, CA: Simile II.

Skutnabb-Kangas, T. (1981). *Bilingualism or not: The education of minorities.* Clevedon, Avon (England): Multilingual Matters.

Snow, C. (1977). The development of conversation between mothers and babies. *Journal of Child Language, 4,* 1–22.

Snow, M. A., Met, M. & Genesee, F. (1989). A conceptual framework for the integration of language and content in second/foreign language instruction. *TESOL Quarterly, 23*(2), 201–217.

Speech therapist who gives and takes accents. (1993, August 11). *The New York Times,* p. A10.

Spolsky, B. (1986). *Language and education in multilingual settings.* San Diego, CA: College-Hill Press.

Spolsky, B., & Cooper, R. L. (Eds.). (1978). *Case studies in bilingual education.* Rowley, MA: Newbury House.

Spradley, J. P. (Ed.). (1972). *Culture and cognition: Rules, maps, and plans.* San Francisco: Chandler.

Spradley, J. P., & McCurdy, D. W. (1972). *The cultural experience: Ethnography in a complex society.* Chicago: Science Research Associates.

Strength through wisdom: A critique of U.S. capability. (1980). *Modern Language Journal, 64,* 9–57.

Study reveals teachers' superstitious beliefs. (1988, September 11). *San Jose Mercury News,* p. 20A.

Suarez-Orozco, M. M., & Suarez-Orozco, C. E. (1993). Hispanic cultural psychology: Implications for teacher education and research. In P. Phelan and A. Locke Davidson (Eds.), *Renegotiating cultural diversity in American schools.* New York: Teachers College Press.

Sue, S., & Padilla, A. (1986). Ethnic minority issues in the United States: Challenges for the educational system. In California State Department of Education (Ed.), *Beyond language: Social and cultural factors in schooling language minority students* (pp. 36–72). Los Angeles: Evaluation, Dissemination and Assessment Center, California State University, Los Angeles.

Tannen, D. (1990). *You just don't understand: Women and men in conversation.* New York: Morrow.

Teitelbaum, H., & Hiller, H. J. (1977). Bilingual education: The legal mandate. *Harvard Educational Review, 47,* 138–170.

Terrell, T. D. (1981). The natural approach in bilingual education. In California State Department of Education (Ed.), *Schooling and language minority students: A theoretical framework* (pp. 117–146). Los Angeles: Evaluation, Dissemination and Assessment Center, California State University, Los Angeles.

Thonis, E. (1983). *The English-Spanish connection.* Northvale, NJ: Santillana.

Tomlinson, E. H., & Eastwick, J. F. (1980). Allons enfants. *Independent School, 40*(1), 23–31.

Trasvina, J. (1981, August 7). Bilingual elections safeguard rights of linguistic minorities. *The Denver Post.*

Trueba, H. T. (Ed.). (1987). *Success or failure? Learning and the language minority student.* Rowley, MA: Newbury House.

Trueba, H. T., Guthrie, G. P., & Au, K. H. (Eds.). (1981). *Culture and the bilingual classroom: Studies in classroom ethnography.* Rowley, MA: Newbury House.

Tyack, D. B. (1974). *The one best system: A history of American urban education.* Cambridge, MA: Harvard University Press.

U.S. Department of Education, Office of the Secretary. (1992). *The condition of bilingual education in the nation: A report to congress and the president, June 30, 1992.* Washington, DC: Government Printing Office.

U.S. General Accounting Office. (1987a). *Bilingual education: A new look at the research evidence* (GAO/PEMD-87-12BR). Washington, DC: Government Printing Office.

U.S. General Accounting Office. (1987b). *Bilingual education: Information on limited English proficient students* (GAO/HRD-87-85BR). Washington, DC: Government Printing Office.

Valdes, J. M. (Ed.). (1986). *Culture bound: Bridging the cultural gap in language teaching.* New York: Cambridge University Press.

Van Horne, W. A., & Tonnesen, T. V. (Eds.). (1987). *Ethnicity and language.* Milwaukee: The University of Wisconsin System Institute on Race and Ethnicity.

Ventriglia, L. (1982). *Conversations with Miguel and Maria: How children learn English as a second language: Implications for classroom teaching.* Reading, MA: Addison-Wesley.

Viadero, D. (1991, November 6). Foreign-language instruction resurfacing in elementary schools. *Education Week,* pp. 1, 12-13.

Voting Rights Act of 1965, as amended, 42 U.S.C. sec. 1973 et seq.

Wang, P. C. (1986). A bilingual education lesson from China. *Thrust, 16*(1), 38-39.

Wardhaugh, R. (1993). *Investigating language: Central problems in linguistics.* Oxford: Basil Blackwell.

Warren-Leubecker, A., & Bohannon J. N. III. (1985). Language in society: Variation and adaptation. In J. B. Gleason (Ed.), *The development of language* (pp. 331-367). Columbus, OH: Merrill.

Weinberg, M. (1977). *A chance to learn: A history of race and education in the United States.* New York: Cambridge University Press.

Wells, S. (1986, July 28). Bilingualism: The accent is on youth. *U.S. News & World Report,* p. 60.

Wesman, A. G. (1969). Intelligent testing. *American Psychologist, 23,* 267-274.

Wilbur, R. (1980). The linguistic description of American sign language. In H. Lane & F. Grosjean (Eds.), *Recent perspectives on American sign language* (pp. 7-31). Hillsdale, NJ: Lawrence Erlbaum Associates.

Williams, J. D., & Capizzi Snipper, G. (1990). *Literacy and bilingualism.* White Plains, NY: Longman.

Willig, A. C. (1985). A meta-analysis of selected studies on the effectiveness of bilingual education. *Review of Educational Research, 55,* 269-317.

Wineburg, S. S. (1987). When good intentions aren't enough. *Phi Delta Kappan, 68,* 544-545.

Wolfson, N., & Manes, J. (Eds.). (1985). *Language of inequality.* Berlin: Mouton.

Wong Fillmore, L. (1985). Second language learning in children: A proposed model. In National Clearinghouse for Bilingual Education (Ed.), *Issues in English language development* (pp. 33-42). Rosslyn, VA: National Clearinghouse for Bilingual Education.

Woolard, K. A. (1985). Catalonia: The dilemma of language rights. In N. Wolfson & J. Manes (Eds.), *Language of inequality* (pp. 91-107). Berlin: Mouton.

# Index

Academic achievement
  autonomous minorities and, 105, 107
  castelike minorities and, 106, 108
  contextual interaction and, 104–105, 108
  cultural deficit and, 100–101
  cultural differences and, 99
  culturally deprived minorities and, 111–112
  cultural mismatch and, 99, 101–104
  genetic inferiority model and, 100
  immigrant minorities and, 105–107
  perceptions of minorities on role of schools and, 107–108
  relationship between bilingualism and, 65–66
  secondary cultural differences and, 106–107
  testing and, 108–111
Ada, Flor, 20
Additive bilingualism
  beneficial nature of, 65
  explanation of, 58
  views regarding, 61
African Americans
  as castelike minorities, 106
  demographics for, 88, 110
Age, language acquisition and, 44
Alternative assessment approaches, 79–80
American G.I. Forum, 119

Antiquity, bilingualism in, 1–2
Asher, James, 74
*Aspira of New York, Inc. v. Board of Education,* 125
Assessment. *See also* Testing; Tests
  of content area instruction combined with language instruction, 79–80
  cultural bias in, 56
  of language ability, 54–57
Assimilation, pluralism versus, 147–148
Assimilationist program models, 12
Audiolingual method, 73–74
Autonomous minorities, 105

Babbling, 41
Banks, James, 20
Basic interpersonal communicative skills (BICS), 54, 64
Basque, 133
Berlitz, Maximilian, 73
Bias
  as concern in assessment, 56, 99
  content and construct, 109–110
Bicognitivism, 102
Biculturalism, 102
Bilingual Crosscultural Language Academic Development/ Crosscultural Language Academic Development (BCLAD/CLAD), 19
Bilingual Education Act (1968)
  expansions of, 121–123

INDEX **169**

interaction style and, 103-104
limitations of, 104
Culture
  demographic factors related to, 88-89
  ethnographic studies of, 101
  explanation of, 89-91
  impact of immigration and, 85, 87-88
  manifestations of, 92-94
  relationship between language and,
    91-92
  theory of oppositional, 106-107
Culture-fair tests, 111
Culture-free tests, 111
Culver City Spanish Immersion Program
  (California), 15
Cummins, Jim, 52-54, 64
Curran, Charles, 75
Curtis, Edward S., 91

Deficiency model, 100-101
Dialects, 32-33
*Diana v. State Board of Education,* 109
Dictation, as measure of language ability,
  55
Differential achievement. *See also*
  Academic achievement
  analysis of, 99
  contextual interaction as solution to, 108
Direct method, 73
Discrete point tests, 54-56
Discrimination
  in language assessment, 56, 99
  against minority war veterans, 119
  in standardized testing, 109-110
Dual language instruction. *See also*
  Second language instruction
  civil rights movement and, 118-120
  connection between multicultural
    and, 21
  desegregation and, 127-128
  for elite groups, 17-18
  federal involvement in, 120-121
  federal legislation regarding, 121-126
  historical background of, 1-7
  mislabeling and misconceptions
    regarding, 66, 71
  research on, 66
  role of paraprofessionals in, 19
  state legislation regarding, 126-127
  World War II and, 118-119
Dual language policy
  explanation of, 131-132
  language suppression and, 133-134
  planning and, 132-133

Dual language programs
  enrichment, 14
  immersion, 14-17
  maintenance, 13-14
  models of, 11-12
  in private schools, 17-18
  transitional, 12-13
Dual language teachers
  credentials for, 18-19
  grants for training of, 122
  requirements for, 18
  support for biliteracy by, 81

Eastman Avenue School (Los Angeles), 13
Echolalic babbling, 41
Education for All Handicapped Children
  Act of 1975, 109
Educational performance. *See* Academic
  achievement
Elementary and Secondary Education Act
  (ESEA), 7, 121, 122
Enculturation, 90
English, as official language, 146
English as a new language (ENL) learners,
  12
English as a second language (ESL)
  programs, 68, 71
English as a second language (ESL)
  teachers, 18-19
English language development (ELD)
  teachers, 18-19
Enrichment programs, 14, 15
Equal Educational Opportunities Act of
  1974, 125-126
Escalante, Jaime, 108
Ethnography, 101

Farsi, 136
Feuerstein, Reuven, 111-112
Field independent students, 101
Field sensitive students, 101-102
*Finding Out/Descubrimiento,* 69
Fishman, Joshua A., 149
Flemish language, 143
Foley, D. E., 106-107
Foreign language instruction
  at elementary level, 136
  impact of isolationism and nationalism
    on, 6
Foreigner-talk, 45
French language, 143

Genetic inferiority, 100
German-Americans, 5-6, 140-141